THE
DESTINY
DESIGNER

7 SACRED FLAMES TO LIGHT YOUR PATH WITH PASSION AND PLAYFUL PROSPERITY

LAUREN PEROTTI

THE DESTINY DESIGNER

Published by:
Transformation Books
211 Pauline Drive #513
York, PA 17402
www.TransformationBooks.com

ISBN # 978-1-945252-18-1
Library of Congress Control No: 2016960232

Cover Design: Ranilo Cabo
Layout and typesetting: Ranilo Cabo
Editor: Michelle Cohen
Proofreader: Michelle Cohen
Midwife: Carrie Jareed

Printed in the United States of America

THE
DESTINY DESIGNER

7 SACRED FLAMES TO LIGHT
YOUR PATH WITH PASSION AND
PLAYFUL PROSPERITY

CONTENTS

DEDICATION

This book is dedicated to all of you who desire more *ALIVENESS* and *LIGHT* in your lives, livelihoods, and the world. It's for you, the dreamer who wants to build your castles in the air onto solid ground. It's for all of you who want to learn and practice how to create a clear vision for your soul dreams and make them manifest in a material, playful, and prosperous way. Finally, it's for you, the visionary who wants to be a vital force in furthering a new era of leadership that allows spirit, imagination, and creativity to inform strategies, decisions, and actions. I'm excited for you to join me in my mission to Light Up The World!

The creation of *The Destiny Designer* was Divinely guided by the same wisdom and practices I present within it. Thanks to my core team of heavenly guides and advisors, especially Archangels Gabriel and Raphael. I also thank God, Jesus, the Holy Spirit, Mary, my ancestors, and the wisdom of the archetypal ages, as well as beloved people right here on this earthly plane that support my vision. I'm grateful for this abundant energy, and it is my deep, driving desire to share it with YOU!

OPENING

You are what your deep, driving desire is.
As your desire is, so is your will.
As your will is, so is your deed. As your deed is,
so is your destiny.
~ *The Brihadaranyaka Upanishad*

Welcome! I'm so glad that some part of you, I'd like to think it was your spirit, felt drawn to pick up this book. It tells me that you are on a quest for a new or revitalized vision for your life, one infused with much more meaning, more aliveness and even more playfulness. It tells me that you desire to choose and design your destiny rather than allow uninspiring circumstances decide your fate. You are also part of a global awakening of consciousness, both personal and collective, that is driving many of us toward living, leading, and working with greater spirit, purpose, passion, integrity, peace, and joy. You are opening to awakening.

On my own path of awakening, I've noticed this wave building for several decades, and it seems to be reaching a crescendo now. All you have to do is browse the Personal and Spiritual Development section at your local bookstore, or on Amazon, to see the abundance of books out there designed to help people transform their lives and livelihoods in this direction. I've found that when the student is ready, a teacher who speaks your particular language appears. I hope my language speaks to you.

In my role as a Life Purpose and *Dream*Builder coach, and even simply in everyday life, so many people from all walks of life have shared their extreme frustration with me about feeling unfulfilled, unheard, underutilized, and unexpressed in their world. I just recently talked to yet another seasoned executive who works in an environment in which she has to check her soul at the door before she walks in, because there's no place or space for its expression there. I also just met a man who is an expert at directing an organization's mission, yet it hadn't occurred to him to create his own personal mission statement and strategic plan. These folks have achieved some level of outward success, though it rings hollow for them on the inside. Like you, they desire more spirit in their success.

It could be that you feel stuck on the treadmill of never-ending responsibilities with no room for playing in your passions—and maybe you don't even know what it is that you are passionate about. Do you find yourself expending a lot of energy meeting others' needs or demands, at the expense of your own wellness and happiness? And even if your life feels relatively satisfying, you could have an unrealized dream inside that you'd love to make real.

The truth is, even when you can perform your job or parenting function with your eyes closed, you can start to lose your soul when you're not fully expressing your genius—those brilliant parts of you that shine with the gifts and honed skills that make you unique. And when that happens for long enough, it can feel as if a part of you is in the dark and dying. Why be alive if you're not really living?

Are you ready to ignite the fire of your
purpose, passion, and power?

Are you ready to discover infinite sources
of energy and light so you can keep your fire
burning more steadily?

Are you ready to free your creative spirit
so you can shine your unique spark of light in the world?

Then I invite you to proclaim:

It is now time to awaken and pursue my
next dream and make it real!

You can start with getting clear about your soul's mission and igniting the fire of your passion and personal power. This book will teach you a creative and spiritual methodology—

The Destiny Designer™–so you can manifest and live your Divine Destiny. This unique process offers several integral components, including Seven Sacred Flames, to give you tools and practices that will not only keep your fire burning, but will help you create a LifePlay Plan in alignment with your purpose. How would you like to create your Soul Song–and sing it? Perhaps you'd rather pen your Purpose Poem, design your Destiny Dance, or make your Mission Masterpiece? These are just some of many ways you can awaken and free your creative spirit so that more of your inner soul is expressed.

Throughout this book, you'll notice I use the word Divine quite often. Divine can mean many different things to each of us, from God to god-like, to universal, to sacred, to delightful, and more. When I talk about this, I am referring to the sacred and universal source that all matter comes from, a source more powerful than you or me. This is beyond any religious concept of God, though I sometimes refer to certain religious or spiritual perspectives of the topics I explore with you. Ultimately, for me, the Divine is a source of Love and Light that is eternal, and from which you and I spark.

Amid all this juicy, creative and mystical work, I still also use my business acumen serving as the Chief Financial and Strategy Officer for a prominent family-owned Napa Valley vineyard and real estate group of companies. The owners I work with are fun, fabulous, and flexible and our relationship is mutually rewarding.

Who Am I to Write This Book?

When I was a very young girl, I was afraid of the dark. Many children have this fear, but mine was not really as much about scary monsters or things of that nature. My fear of darkness came from feeling on my own, disconnected from the light of my essence. Even though my large Italian-American family was the source of lots of love and blessings, I somehow still felt as if there were a missing part of me that left a dark hole inside. I remember sometimes wondering, "Why am I here?" With this disconnect, I made many life choices, including my primary career path and relationship, that I later came to understand did not allow for my fully alive, creative expression. This feeling stirred in me my lifelong quest to look for the light that could fill that black hole and illuminate my particular path to Oz.

What is this light I am talking about? As I've discovered through my many life trials, it's the light of spirit that never goes out. It's the light that comes from awareness and wisdom, from deep connection to others, and ultimately from knowing, expressing, serving, and living my life purpose with a sense of fun, creativity, and playfulness. Life does not have to be so hard. The good news is that it could be a lot easier for you.

I've been there and—though I had buried that black hole I felt as a young girl—I eventually had the opportunity, the choice to face it again. That's how I eventually found my purpose and passion. And one of my passions is to guide others like you to discover yours—professional or otherwise.

As a young woman, I discovered that, because of my childhood family patterns, my self-identity unconsciously came from other people, places, and things. By that time, I was seemingly thriving as a senior manager in an international accounting firm, living in a beautiful Newport Beach townhouse, and looking successful. I had climbed that corporate ladder quickly and was primed for a promotion to partner in the firm.

I had already gone through the crumbling of my alcoholic marriage, which made me painfully aware again of that black hole. The pain was so intense that, since then, I had spent several years on my own personal development quest; I engaged in psychotherapy, spiritual, and personality assessment systems, and even a 12-step program for co-dependency. I had uncovered and healed some childhood wounds and had begun to work on others. Through all of this, I got a sense of who I really was and the life I'd love to be living. I was waking up.

With that awakening came my increasing discontent with the deadline-driven demands of that career, which kept me focused on meeting and exceeding others' needs and expectations at my own expense. This environment mirrored that of my childhood family, in which my role, in part, was to create order out of emotional chaos. My life was out of balance, and I wasn't engaging enough in my passions–singing, the arts, spirituality, and adventure quests to name a few. Although there were ways I felt satisfied in this career, there were too many of my talents that were being

. . . .

suppressed. I thirsted for something more meaningful, but I felt STUCK. I kept on running that rat race because I saw no viable way out.

So what happened? My body failed—and bailed me out. I started feeling run down, but convinced myself I was working too hard and just needed a break. Pretty quickly, my symptoms grew—fevers and night sweats, lightheadedness—to the point of nearly fainting and unexplained bruises. Clearly something was wrong, but I still kept on running that race, caught in the world of ten thousand things.

While at an out-of-town conference, I happened to brush my leg against a table, which immediately brought up a huge, hard and black bruise. Now I was scared. When I got back to my hotel room that evening, I stared in the mirror at my pale face and bruised body and couldn't ignore this any longer. I took myself to the emergency room, where I was shockingly diagnosed with Acute Leukemia.

My dis-ease had seeped down to the core of my bones, into the marrow and was surging through my blood!

So began another transforming journey. I spent the better part of that year in hospitalized isolation, connected 24/7 to a surgically implanted catheter in my chest that was being infused with large volumes of nuclear-level chemo, blood, antibiotics, and more that I needed to sustain my life. I could not leave the room or detach from the IV pole. Yet, paradoxically, after the initial shock of the diagnosis, instead of feeling stuck, I was freer and more joyful than I had ever been.

How could this be true? Wouldn't such a physical and existential trial be like a wild rollercoaster ride through pain and fear, to hope, to doubt, and back up again for any human being, especially over such a long time period? Would I live or die? At times, my body felt nearly as ravaged by my harrowing treatment as that of Jesus Christ at his crucifixion, with whom I identified during this journey that began near Eastertime. Just as he shed his blood for our salvation, my own blood was being purified for MY redemption–and a new life. Therein laid my hope, and with hope comes light.

Other factors helped me reach for the light amid dark moments. First, I was connected to a community and surrounded by waves of love that touched and infused me. It's important to note that I started this wave by immediately informing people about my plight, rather than keeping it a secret. When these people rapidly spread the word, the wave expanded outward in ever widening circles, like those created when you toss a pebble into a pond. The waves that circled back around me came from family, friends, neighbors, owners of businesses I patronized, my team of doctors, Jesus and the Angels, and even business colleagues from the very firm I had been trying so hard to leave! I openly absorbed the love, and literally felt myself vibrating at a higher level. I have found that love is the vibration that elicits healing and joy. I talk about the power of Love as a universal source of energy and light in Chapter Five.

Second, being isolated gave me the opportunity to practice something I first learned in the Al-anon 12-step program—how to live one day at a time and become acutely present in the here and now. This is, after all, where the kingdom of heaven truly resides. Here I was, high-energy, social, and claustrophobic to boot, forced into seclusion with no choice but to finally slow down. Instead of feeling sorry for myself with what could have felt like a cosmic joke, I considered this an opportunity to grow. When I was enduring some of the most grueling, painful things imaginable that happened to my body from my treatment, I reminded myself that this, too, would pass. Any time I began to think too much about feeling trapped or future-trip about whether I would live or die, I chose instead to journal, pray, talk to someone, or watch something funny on the television. Even gazing out my window was a practice in staying in the beauty of the moment. Presence is the first of the Seven Sacred Flames I talk about in Chapter Six.

Third, I transformed what could have been a sterile hospital room into a studio for life-giving creativity—music, singing, and art. This required some negotiating on my part—something at which I excel—since my health care team was not accustomed to any patient not simply complying with their protocol without question. With the okay from my health care team, my friends brought over a music player, art materials, and other personal things from my home to decorate this space. Whenever I received gifts and cards from people, I used them to further enhance the aesthetic of my little healing cove by taping them on the walls. The nurses and doctors came around just to see how my colorful place was coming along. I journaled, colored, played music, and sang from the core of my being, and I discovered my truth–that I am a creative, passionate lightworker who also happens to have savvy business and finance acumen. I can and do work with both of these seemingly different aspects of my whole Self.

Finally, deep down, I knew that my very survival depended on loving myself enough to fully forgive and release past hurts, claim my life purpose, and live my passion. I did not want to die with my song, my purpose, still in me before I could fully express it! This resolve, and the blessing of the pioneering, passionate blood of my Italian ancestry, activated the resurrecting power in me.

Now I was ready to live the life I envisioned and step confidently in the direction of my dreams, just as Thoreau suggested in his book *Walden; or, Life in the Woods*. All I needed to do was try! Thoreau's book is about truths he discovered in his experiment to live deliberately, which he did for about two years at Walden Pond. I talk about this in more depth in Chapter Seven of this book. Just as he found for himself, once I took some leap-of-faith steps, all sorts of things began to occur that never otherwise would have. It's really quite magical, in hindsight.

With a spiritual stirring from my core team, I boldly sold nearly everything I owned and moved to the San

Francisco Bay area. My team included both heavenly and earthly beings–close friends, my Al-anon sponsor, Angels, the Holy Spirit, and even Jesus. Certain people thought my spontaneous exodus was crazy. I didn't have a concrete plan or "job," and I only knew a handful of people there. Why would I leave my beautiful Newport Beach place, the warm, sunny beach, and such a supportive community of people to embark into such unknown? I had courage and faith in my inner knowing–I was being called to further serve my soul mission. I chose to say, *yes*. Like Don Quixote, this was my quest, to follow that star.

Soon after I settled into my new digs, I began to talk to just about everyone I met about my passion for the healing and transforming power of creativity. Through those conversations, someone pointed me to a graduate school program that was about just that. Even though I had not intended to go back to school, I again trusted my inner knowing and chose to say, *yes*. I took another step in the direction of my dream. Three rigorous and personally deepening, as well as financially exhausting, years later, I earned a double master's degree in psychology and expressive arts therapy that blended theories of psychology, phenomenology, philosophy, the arts, and spirituality. While it depleted my financial resources, it filled me up with so much wisdom.

For quite a while, I chose to pursue the path to becoming a licensed therapist, which required at least three thousand hours of clinical mental health work with individuals, families, and children, along with ultimately passing two exams. I did all this while earning a fraction of what I used to make in my old world. It was mostly fulfilling, challenging, and everything in between. However, when it came time to finally take the second of the licensing exams, I decided this was not quite right for my soul mission and after much consternation, chose not to take this final step. "What?! Are you nuts? After all that, you're not going to get licensed?" That was the response I got from many.

It's not as if I hadn't already noticed my subtle discontent on this licensure path numerous times along the way. But I kept telling myself that I had already come this far, so why not just get the license, just in case I wanted to practice as a licensed therapist here and there while mostly doing life coaching. When I finally stood at this turning point, I realized that to continue along half committed was akin to what recovering alcoholics call holding on to old ideas. The result you really desire, they say, will be nil until you let go absolutely. If I stand for doing what my soul is here to express, why would I continue to follow a path that wasn't quite right for me, especially if I guide you to do the same? This was a momentous soul decision. It was time for me to release myself from this obligation.

How did I do so? Two of my soul sisters, who earned that same degree alongside me, actually did understand. We staged a ritual at an outdoor fire pit by the bay where I named and affirmed all the gifts, knowledge, and experience that I was taking with me, and that I was letting go. Then I calmly and confidently tossed all the paperwork that I had needed to accumulate for the Board of Behavioral Sciences into the pit. As I watched the flames burn it up, I felt liberated and on fire for what was next. I knew that I was truly more of a coach. The art of ritual and the element of fire are both potent ingredients for transformation, as you will read about in Chapter Six where I introduce you to the Seven Sacred Flames.

With my coach purpose in my thoughts, I was then led through serendipity to study Life Mastery programs with Mary Morrissey, a world-renowned life coach, motivational speaker, spiritual author, and Founder of Life Mastery Institute. I resonated so much with Mary's spirit, her philosophy, and her over forty years of experience in the new thought milieu that I became certified as an LMI *Dream*Builder Coach. This gave me yet more tools to guide you to create your ideal life with the art and science of success.

Soon thereafter, I discovered and learned one of the most profound methodologies through which to discover and understand specific life purpose. Soul Purpose Hand Analysis, which I talk about more in Chapter One, combines the art of palmistry with the science of fingerprints to decode your soul's blueprint in your hands.

Most recently, I have deepened my spiritual knowledge and capacities by studying with Doreen Virtue, a renowned Angel Therapist, and became certified as an Angel Card Reader. As you'll discover later in this book, this is one of many powerful tools available for you to connect with your highest vision.

Why Am I Writing This Book Now?

With all this potency in my hands, I felt inspired to integrate these elements together into a powerful process to guide others like you to make your life a masterpiece. That's why and when I created my signature program, The Destiny Designer™. As I said earlier, it's a multi-faceted methodology for you to discover, design, live, and lead your Spirit-inspired life and livelihood with joy, authentic and creative expression, and playful prosperity. The process guides you to be more energized, empowered, and enlightened by giving you New Ways to Play in your life, because when you change your thoughts and habits, you will change your life.

The Destiny Designer™ synthesizes wisdom and practices from chakra energy and light channels, nature's elements, angelic guidance, creative arts processes, and symbolic and archetypal imagery. It also provides a practical and structured template for you to create your new LifePlay Plan. Some of these sources are universal and scientific in nature, while others are based on the formed knowledge of experts with whom I have studied and collaborated. I channel this knowledge through my own lens of understanding, experience, and intuitive guidance.

You and I play a unique part in the mighty orchestra of the universe. Isn't it time to make your life a masterpiece?

With this book you will:

- Create a personal mission statement and LifePlay Plan in alignment with your Soul purpose.
- Discover YOUR kingdom of heaven that is available in the here and now.
- Free your creative spirit–tap your imagination, play, create, and recreate.
- Hone your authentic voice and speak your truth with confidence in any situation.
- Shift your thinking and perceptions for greater clarity and decision-making.
- Create a clear vision of a life you LOVE and manifest it into reality.

Ultimately, this book will inspire you to march confidently in the direction of your dreams. Along the way, you'll discover your richest source of prosperity and have much more fun.

Here's to making your life a masterpiece! Let's go!

Lauren

PART ONE

*S*park Your Inner Fire

There is a fire inside. Sit down beside it. Watch the flames,
the ancient, flickering dance of yourself.
~ John MacEnulty

CHAPTER ONE

PIECE TOGETHER YOUR DIVINE PURPOSE PUZZLE

Tell your heart that the fear of suffering is worse than the suffering itself. And that no heart has ever suffered when it goes in search of its dreams, because every second of the search is a second's encounter with God and with eternity.

~ Paulo Coelho

Would you rather be a lump of coal or a diamond? I've always proclaimed that I want to be a diamond, bright, shiny, and even a little sparkly. The truth is, we are each like a diamond—unique, multi-faceted, and designed to receive and reflect light. Just as it takes tremendous heat and pressure deep in the earth to transform carbon into a brilliant natural diamond, sometimes your highest human potential comes through dark times and fiery trials. Can you use your stress and darkness to be a catalyst to ignite your resurrecting purpose, passion, and power within?

The Talmud, a sacred ancient and core text of Rabbinic Judaism, says that, "Every blade of grass has its angel that bends over it and whispers, 'Grow, grow.'" Just imagine what that blade of grass must do in order to keep growing and rising–pressing through soil, even cement, to seek the light. Haven't we all seen a blade of grass pushing its way through a sidewalk crack? What a seemingly hard task! Sometimes our human quest to live more of who we really are and do more of what we love can feel that hard.

What if you are just like that blade of grass, designed to reach for the light, to desire more growth, and more expression of what is in your DNA? And what if you, too, have an angel that bends over you, encouraging you to rise up and reflect your light?

Your very DNA is shaped in a spiral, and you live in a spiral universe that is ever expanding–is this a coincidence? We are each a spark of the Universe, which is our extended body; this is not merely a lofty notion, but an immutable law of physics–the Law of Divine Oneness. If every element and being in the universe has a unique purpose, so, too, do you and I. The more you understand your divine self and, better yet, develop and maintain a connection to and then align your life path with it, the more the universe and everything and everyone around you will empower your ability to manifest your greatest dreams along the way. As Steve Winwood sings,

It's time to reach for the light, come out of the darkness and find out who you are.

Maybe you think that you should already know who you are and why you are here, especially if you're someone who has achieved a high level of executive functioning. Yet, you'd be amazed at how many adults, who otherwise seem to have it all together, can't answer that question with clarity. Why is that? Perhaps when your focus is on the outside, it becomes natural to place your meaning there. You can go about the tasks of daily living on autopilot, without questioning things too deeply. When you're busy with the responsibilities of jobs, spouses, kids, and community involvements, you can lose connection to self.

That was true for me. Even though I could attach my identity to my title, or my image, or my relationship status, it took some time for me to find the personal development tools that helped me discover my deeper soul purpose. And I had to do this before I could paint a vivid picture of my passion and my dreams, much less feel empowered to live in a new way. In the meantime, it was much easier for me to write a strategic business plan for an organization than to create my own personal mission statement and spirit-driven life plan.

Your autopilot might look like this: Wake up, get the kids ready for school, go to work, hit the grocery store or the gym, come home and make dinner, help the kids with their homework, get them to bed, prepare for tomorrow's meetings, collapse. Wash, Rinse, Repeat. Even if you don't have children, other iterations of this picture set in and before you know it, days, weeks, months, and years are flying by in a blur.

You may go to some kind of church every Sunday, or on holidays, but too often it may be out of some sense of conditioned obligation and does not fulfill your soul's deepest longing. You may not take the time otherwise, or even know how, to connect with something greater than yourself, or you're too busy to make it a regular practice.

Life might even look really good on the outside, but eventually it feels hollow on the inside when you're not connected to a deeper sense of meaning or your mission. If this rings true for you, you're not alone. Many people live this way, without realizing they're not happy or fulfilled. I've heard it said that some people live ninety years while others live the same year ninety times.

The good news is that you can choose your destiny rather than merely accept your fate. Awareness is the one of the first keys to awakening, because, of course, you can't change anything until you are aware of it. An ancient Greek maxim is, "Know thyself"! How can you do so, and where can you begin? The following sections will show you how you can piece together your divine purpose puzzle using a potpourri of resources.

Understanding Your Self

There are so many tools, processes, and perspectives available for gaining a deeper understanding about your essential nature, which consists of your personality, soul, and spirit. You may wonder what the difference is between these aspects of self, and many have pondered this question from spiritual, psychological, philosophical and even scientific perspectives for thousands of years, and still today. It's a human quest.

The belief system with which I most resonate considers your spirit to be your innermost essence as energy. It's like at your core, you are a local address for a unique spark of the Divine. How is this different from your soul? I agree with others who characterize your soul as that part of you that mentally drives your spirit through your particular conscience, ideals, and intuition. Your personality is how your soul expresses itself through the ego's functioning (feelings, thoughts, and character traits). All of these facets are housed in your physical body, which is why it is also essential for you to take care of this sanctuary in order to live in full expression of all of you. Your purpose is an inner aspect of who you are and an outer expression of what you've come here to express and do.

If you're at the beginning of your discovery journey—or at any time, really—it can be very informative to use some assessment tools for expanding your awareness of your personality character and how you operate. Here are a few of the many self-discovery tools now available, which I have used and studied. My discussion here is not intended to be a complete tutorial of these systems, but more of a synthesizing summary for you. Still, it may seem that there is a lot of information here to metabolize, and I encourage you to take it in at your own pace.

For those of you who come from a Catholic background or any other upbringing that forbids the use of divination devices, let me assure you that while some may use these systems for predicting forthcoming events, many others like me do not seek to foretell the future through them. Rather, these tools provide a psychosocial lens on personal nature that can help you get a clearer understanding of your preferred modes so that you can align your ways with your human design. I share here about those that were instrumental for me to piece together my own divine purpose puzzle.

Myers-Briggs Type Indicator (MBTI®)

This personality assessment measures psychological preferences in how you energize, perceive the world, make decisions, and structure your daily life. They were based on theories proposed by Carl Jung. He defined four main psychological functions by which we experience the world: sensation, intuition, feeling, and thinking.

Isabel Briggs Myers and her mother, Katharine Briggs, developed the MBTI® system in order to make Jung's insights of type theory accessible to the masses. The system describes sixteen separate personality types and profiles based on your preferences in each of four dimensions–introversion/extraversion, intuition/sensing, feeling/thinking, and perceiving/judging.[1]

While some of you may stay fairly anchored on one end of the continuum or the other, in any or all of these areas, others of you tend to fall on a middle ground between them. If so, you may relate to more than one of the personality profiles, just as you may be on the cusp of two astrological signs. When you look at this grid below, can you determine where your preference lies in each of the four dimensions?

THE PREFERENCE POLARITIES	
How you energize	
Introverted (I) Reflective Receptive Intimate	**Extroverted (E)** Expansive Initiative Social
How you perceive the world	
Intuition (N) Visionary Idealistic Conceptual	**Sensing (S)** Concrete Realistic Practical
How you make decisions	
Feeling (F) Emotional Compassionate Subjective	**Thinking (T)** Analytical Logical Objective
How you structure your life	
Perceiving (P) Open-ended Non-linear Spontaneous	**Judging (J)** Decisive Organized Scheduled

You don't have to be shy to prefer alone time for refueling, and you can really like socializing even if you're not overly outgoing. It's also possible to have strengths in one area even though you prefer to operate on the opposite side of it. For example, supposing you prefer to structure your life in an open-ended way, you may still be able to act in a decisive way in some areas of your life, especially if you are a business professional.

If you actually take the MBTI® assessment quiz available on the Myers and Briggs Foundation website, you will find out which of these sixteen personality types most represents you.[2] Even if you don't take that step, you can hone in on your profile by first finding your preferences and then reviewing the following grid, which I created based on my understanding of the types.

LIVE IN THE POTENTIAL			
INFJ **The Signifi-cance Seeker** Insightful, inspiring, and introspective	**ENFJ** **The Motivating Mobilizer** Empowering, engaging, and empathic	**INTJ** **The Improvement Implementer** Imaginative, innovative, and independent	**ENTJ** **The Strategic Spearhead** Planning, procedural, and presenting
INFP **The Inspired Idealist** Implementing ideas and loyal	**ENFP** **The Charismatic Catalyst** Captivating, connecting, and creative	**INTP** **The Problem-Solving Professor** Analytical, abstract , and adaptable	**ENTP** **The Ingenious Inventor** Conceptual, challenging, and clever

LIVE IN THE PRESENT			
ISFJ **The** **Dedicated** **Doer** Committed, considerate, and conscientious	**ESFJ** **The** **Harmonizing** **Host** Cooperative, considerate, and congenial	**ISTJ** **The Orderly** **Organizer** Realistic, reliable, and responsible	**ESTJ** **The** **Organizing** **Orchestrator** Decisive, driving, and efficient
ISFP **The Artistic** **Arranger** Aesthetic, ecstatic, and activist	**ESFP** **The Sociable** **Star** Flexible, friendly, and fun	**ISTP** **The** **Enigmatic** **Engineer** Physical, practical, and problem-solving	**ESTP** **The** **Spontaneous** **Straight-** **Shooter** Energetic, executing, and experiential

When I first discovered my ENFP personality profile through this lens–what I've dubbed The Charismatic Catalyzer–it opened my awareness to who I really was. The woman who administered my MBTI® assessment assured me that my misery in my work world was completely understandable given my nature. In fact, she was astounded that I had endured as many years at it as I had. I remember crying because someone else validated and verbalized what I had started to realize. I wasn't crazy. I know so many people who also felt awakened and assured by understanding their MBTI® profiles.

Numerology

If you are a numbers person—and hopefully, even if you're not—you will love using this tool to discover more about your nature and your life path. Dating back thousands of years, numerology is the study of the powerful symbolism and cosmic vibration of numbers as they can point to your strengths, talents, and overall life path. Each number from 1 to 9, as well as the Master numbers of 11, 22, and 33, are seen as having their own unique character essence; and as with the other personality systems, even though some life path profiles may share similar character traits, they still differ from one another. Master numbers have extra potency, with more potential and more challenges.

Many ancient philosophers, including Pythagoras and Saint Augustine, considered numbers a universal language given to us by God. They believed that all things have numerical significance and that we can use our own mental faculties to explore these relationships or ask for divine understanding of them.

Unfortunately, the early Christian church authorities did not approve of the use of foretelling, and the study of the sacredness of numbers joined the ranks of astrology and other practices that were seen as dark magic diverting us away from solely seeking God's wisdom. Ironically, there are multitudes of overt numerical references in the Bible, as well as in other spiritual teachings. There are so many, and it is so fascinating to me, that I could write a book solely on this topic. For now, I'll mention a few examples that stand out.

The number twelve is found throughout the Bible. There are twelve tribes of Israel, also referenced in Judaism and in the Islamic Quran. Jesus chose twelve disciples who later became apostles. After Jesus miraculously fed the five thousand people, who had gathered in the desert to hear his message with five loaves of bread and two fish as told in Matthew 14:13-21, the disciples picked up twelve baskets of food that remained. This number is also profoundly symbolic throughout the book of Revelations, particularly its description of the City of Heaven:

"And he carried me away in the spirit to a great and high mountain, and showed me that great city, the holy Jerusalem, descending out of heaven from God, Having the glory of God: and her light was like unto a stone most precious, even like a jasper stone, clear as crystal; And had a wall great and high, and had twelve gates, and at the gates twelve angels, and names written thereon, which are the names of the twelve tribes of the children of Israel: On the east three gates; on the north three gates; on the south three gates; and on the west three gates. And the wall of the city had twelve foundations, and in them the names of the twelve apostles of the Lamb. And he that talked with me had a golden reed to measure the city, and the gates thereof, and the wall thereof. And the city lieth foursquare, and the length is as large as the breadth: and he measured the city with the reed, twelve thousand furlongs. The length and the breadth and the height of it are equal. And he measured the wall thereof, an hundred and forty and four cubits, according to the measure of a man, that is, of the angel. And the building of the wall of it was of jasper: and the city was pure gold, like unto clear glass. And the foundations of the wall of the city were garnished with all manner of precious stones. The first foundation was jasper; the second, sapphire; the third, a chalcedony; the fourth, an emerald; The fifth, sardonyx; the sixth, sardius; the seventh, chrysolyte; the eighth, beryl; the ninth, a topaz; the tenth, a chrysoprasus; the eleventh, a jacinth; the twelfth, an amethyst. And the twelve gates were twelve pearls: every several gate was of one pearl: and the street of the city was pure gold, as it were transparent glass. And I saw no temple therein: for the Lord God Almighty and the Lamb are the temple of it. And the city had no need of the sun, neither of the moon, to shine in it: for the glory of God did lighten it, and the Lamb is the light thereof."[3]

Notice that the Four Noble Truths and Eight Fold Path of Buddhism totals twelve, which also depicts its twelve stages in the wheel of life. There are twelve signs of the zodiac and months in our calendar year.

The number twelve reduces to the number three in Numerology, which also shows up in the Bible, most notably to represent the Holy Trinity (Father, Son, and Holy Spirit).

Jesus fell under the cross three times, he was crucified when he was thirty-three years old, and he rose from the dead on the third day. This number carries the energetic meaning of wholeness and creation, and that carries into its essence in Numerology.

How does Numerology work? In this system, your birth date or your full birth name generates a variety of personal profiles, most significantly your Life Path, which describes your overall character, life direction, and possibilities for you. Your Life Path number results from adding together the numbers in your full birthdate.

First you add the numbers of your month, date, and year of birth together, reducing each component to a single digit. Then you simply add those three single numbers together and reduce that result to a single digit. For example, if your birthdate is January 1, 1961, your Life Path number is 1 because 1 + 1 + 8 (1 + 9 + 6 + 1 = 17 and 1 + 7 = 8) totals 10 and is reduced to 1.

But if your birthdate were January 20, 1961 your Life Path Number is 11, because 1 + 2 + 8 = 11, which is a Master number that is not reduced. Obviously, it's pretty simple to calculate, and there are even websites that have a calculator right on them for you to use.[4]

When you read the Life Path profiles summarized below, with which do you most relate? And, is this the Life Path number calculated based on your birthdate?

Numerology Life Paths		
Life Path	Personality Type	Keywords
1	The Limelight Leader	Commanding and pioneering trailblazer
2	The Persuasive Peacemaker	Peaceful and harmonizing connector
3	The Creative Communicator	Positive and conversational artist
4	The Community Cornerstone	Practical and decisive builder
5	The Spirit of Change Catalyst	Free-spirited and adventurous life-quester
6	The Healing Helper	Compassionate and healing helper
7	The Smart Spirit Seeker	Spiritual truth seeker and synthesizer
8	The Willful Wealthbuilder	Visionary and authoritative wealth manager
9	The Honorable Humanitarian	Philanthropic and conscious beautifier
11	The Intuitive Illuminator	Spiritual and sensitive, deep thinker
22	The Humanity Herald	Spiritual and practical builder
33	The Christ Consciousness Teacher	Altruistic and loving do-gooder

Enneagram of Personality

The origins of this method for self-understanding and development are still in question, and there are many who write about and teach it. The most well-known experts on this system are Riso and Hudson, who developed The Enneagram Type Indicator. The summarized information I present here is adapted from The Enneagram Institute. It's based on nine interconnected personality types, represented by the points of a geometric figure called an enneagram. We all have aspects of each type within our personality, but are born with one dominant type that influences how we adapt and develop through life.[5]

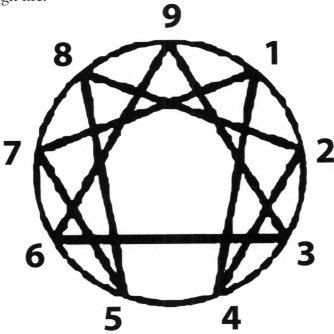

Depending on your enneagram personality type, you are centered in either your Instinct, Thinking, or Feeling, based primarily on your strengths (body, mind, or spirit oriented) and on your unconscious dominant emotional response that comes up when you lose connection to your core self.

Your basic enneagram personality type is complemented by the nature of one of the two that are adjacent to yours on each side of the enneagram diagram (wings), which adds a second dimension to your character. If you are a type nine, you may have strong flavors of either type eight or type one. Each type tends to move toward the behaviors of another point of the enneagram in times of stress or in the opposite direction in periods of growth. For example, an enthusiastic seven may become perfectionistic-like type one when stressed, and yet he can integrate type five's ability to focus in times of growth.

You may wonder how meaningful this system can be when it might boil down every person on the planet into one of nine personality types? The enneagram is more comprehensive than it may seem. Besides the additional intricacy that the wings and directions provide, Riso and Hudson discovered nine levels of development from unhealthy pathology to healthy liberation for each of the nine types and synthesized this into the enneagram system. Still, it is awakening to simply begin with identifying your type. You can take the test to more accurately identify that at the website for The Enneagram Institute, as well as review the summary information here.

The Enneagram Institute describes the nature and characteristics of each of the personality types in detail and also uses these defining type names. Can you relate to one of these?

THE ENNEAGRAM PERSONALITIES			
Personality Type	Center	Dominant Emotion in Stress	Keywords
One The Reformer	Instinctive	Anger	Wise, principled, and purposeful perfectionist
Two The Helper	Feeling	Shame	Loving, caretaking, and people-pleasing giver
Three The Achiever	Feeling	Shame	Effective, driven, and image-conscious performer
Four The Individualist	Feeling	Shame	Original, expressive, and dramatic dreamer
Five The Investigator	Thinking	Fear	Wise, perceptive, and isolated innovator
Six The Loyalist	Thinking	Fear	Responsible, engaging, and eager advocate
Seven The Enthusiast	Thinking	Fear	Joyful, spontaneous, and adventurous epicure
Eight The Challenger	Instinctive	Anger	Heroic, decisive, and dominant boss
Nine The Peacemaker	Instinctive	Anger	Serene, receptive, and reassuring mediator

Astrology

This is yet another lens through which to gain understanding about yourself. When someone mentions astrology, do you roll your eyes and think of a stereotypical, generalized horoscope reading in a newspaper or magazine? The ancient study of astrology is much more complex than most people realize. It's the study of movements and relative positions of celestial bodies and the interpreted influence they have on our bodies, lives, and the natural world—now and at the time of our birth. While there are many skeptics, who view this system of astrology as pseudo-science, the study and practice of looking to the sky in search of human meaning can be traced back thousands of years to the time of cave dwellers who depicted lunar cycles on cave walls.

A natal astrology chart will show the location of the Sun, Moon, and other planets at the time of your birth and can provide very elaborate information about your nature. Even without a full natal chart reading, you can glean some factors that influence your essential self based on your Sun sign of the zodiac according to your birthdate.

Here's a simple chart of summary information about each Sun sign of the zodiac with keyword characteristics about each.[6]

Astrological Sun Signs of the Zodiac				
Sun sign	**Birthdate**	**Symbol**	**Element**	**Keywords**
Aries	Mar 21 - Apr 20	Ram	Fire	Optimistic and pioneering leader
Taurus	Apr 21 - May 21	Bull	Earth	Dependable and prosperous partner
Gemini	May 22 - Jun 21	Twins	Air	Sociable and flexible communicator
Cancer	Jun 22 - Jul 22	Crab	Water	Protective and sensitive nurturer
Leo	Jul 23 - Aug21	Lion	Fire	Warm and courageous leader
Virgo	Aug 22 - Sep 23	Virgin	Earth	Discerning and analytical systematizer
Libra	Sep 24 - Oct 23	Scales	Air	Balancing and refined diplomat
Scorpio	Oct 24 – Nov 22	Scorpion	Water	Mysterious and magnetic
Sagittarius	Nov 23 - Dec 22	Centaur	Fire	Adventurous and outspoken idealist
Capricorn	Dec 23 - Jan 20	Goat	Earth	Ambitious and striving achiever

| Aquarius | Jan 21 - Feb 19 | Water-bearer | Air | Independent and free-spirited helper |
| Pisces | Feb 20- Mar 20 | Fish | Water | Adaptable and imaginative dreamer |

Understanding Your Soul's Mission

When you hear the old saying, "Your life is in your hands," you probably haven't taken it as a literal truth. What if it is true that your soul actually chose a purpose or mission for you to serve, along with the significant life theme and lessons you would face and learn in this lifetime, before you were born—and embossed a blueprint of it on your hands? I've found a system that shows just that. It's one of the most powerful resources I've studied and used for myself and for others in discovering and designing Divine destiny.

This methodology combines ancient palmistry with the latest scientific data about fingerprint identification and advances in human psychology and philosophy. Unlike some forms of palmistry, which predict events in your future life, this method of hand analysis is used as a very specific lens through which to deeply understand these aspects of your soul and specific gifts you may also have to further serve your mission. The Bible and other religions do have something to say about what the hands represent in serving God, and those messages are not substantially different from this perspective.

Richard Unger, who studied fingerprints for nearly fifty years, developed this intricate roadmap for decoding the blueprint of your soul psychology in your hands. Through his reading and studying everything ever written about hands and fingerprints from the world's libraries, and also interviewing thousands of people and analyzing their hands, he discovered patterns that could be discerned in our hands. He laid this out in his book *LIFEPRINTS* and also founded the International Institute of Hand Analysis.[7] I trained directly with Pamelah Landers and Baeth Davis, who both intensively studied and worked with Richard, and I've been giving readings for people now for several years. The results have been transforming and validating for them.

Your fingerprint types, which were imprinted on your hands while you were in utero, are the most uniquely identifying markers for you—even more specific than your DNA. How does anyone know this? Identical twins have the same DNA, but different fingerprints. The primary recognized types include Whorls, Loops, Tented Arches and Arches, along with a few hybrid versions.

In the science of fingerprints, each type is given a ranking value depending on its complexity. As you may be able to discern from looking at these images of each fingerprint type, a Whorl is the most elaborate and has the highest rank, while an Arch is less complex and has the lowest rank among them.[8] This is not a value judgment about which types are more important but simply which required more energy in their creation! The American Academy of Hand Analysis website offers articles, information about research in this field, and images of fingerprints.[9]

Whorl School of Service	Loop School of Love	Tented Arch School of Wisdom	Arch School of Peace

The particular types of fingerprints you have and the digits or thumb on which they lie determine your Life School, Life Purpose, and Life Lesson.

Life School

Imagine your life school as your soul's preparation program, designed to help you develop the skills you will need to fulfill your life purpose. There are four schools, based on the predominant number of fingerprint patterns. Most of you will fall into one of these schools, while other souls have signed up for two or more life schools. Perhaps those souls are trying to expedite their awakening in this lifetime? In any case, your school defines the overall theme of your life.

School of Service (Air element) - If you have Whorls on at least three fingers, then you are here to become a master of service consciousness through communication, teaching, and relaying ideas. You are here to learn how to serve yourself without self-indulgence before you can be of true joyful service in the world without obligation or servitude. [10]

School of Love (Water element) – You need to have at least seven Loops to have enrolled in this training academy. If Love is your school, you are here to overcome whatever obstacles may exist in feeling and expressing your genuine emotional self. When you develop emotional clarity, authenticity, and self-acceptance in relationships rather than explode or stuff your feelings, your purpose will blossom in all areas of your life.[11]

School of Wisdom (Fire element) – With at least two Tented Arches, you chose to learn how to use your wisdom to jump off the fence and risk being fully alive. This involves developing your ability to make decisions and assume leadership. When you ignite your fire to take decisive action instead of react in reckless ways or sit on the fence and go nowhere, you will actually move forward.[12]

School of Peace (Earth element) – If your soul enrolled in this school, which only required one Arch, you are ready to develop a deep sense of inner serenity rather than feel states of panic or paralysis in your body. When you can learn to get grounded and master handling responsibilities without creating urgent crises that distract your attention, you will stop spinning in circles and advance in the direction of your dream.[13]

Life Purpose

This is your soul's contract for your divine mission and represents a consciousness of being rather than a specific role or direction. The finger or thumb that has your highest-ranking fingerprint(s) defines your life purpose.[14]

Your right hand represents your self in the outer world, while your left hand relates to your personal life. Each digit on either hand carries the symbolic meaning of these particular archetypes:

Thumb   Manifestation
Index finger   Leadership, Power, and Vision
Middle finger   Values
Ring finger   Creativity and Arts
Pinky finger   Communications and Connection

For example, if your right index finger carries your print type with the highest value, then your soul purpose involves worldly power, leadership, and empowering others through vision.

Life Lesson

The finger or thumb that has your lowest-ranking fingerprint(s) indicates your life lesson. This represents an aspect of you that is your weak or vulnerable spot; it's often hard to see and it can keep tripping you up until you become aware of it. Once you do, you can turn it into your ally, and it will become the key to your life purpose flourishing.[15]

Let's say your right index finger has your lowest ranking print, with a different finger as your life purpose. Your life lesson would then relate to overcoming how you might be feeling powerless, overwhelmed, or trapped. You may tend to fear that you don't have enough of what life asks of you—either blaming others or even life in general—for your problems. This life lesson will become your friend when you realize that you act in victim-like ways and give away your personal power. Instead, you could reframe your thinking to reclaim your power and inner-authority by incorporating practices that would help strengthen this aspect of your self in order to more fully serve your life purpose (see Chapter Three).

Gift Markers

You may have one or more additional markings on your palms that point to more ways your life purpose can be expressed. This is not to say that those of you who don't have any gift markers on your hands don't have fabulous talents, or that you aren't already expressing any of these special skills in your life. But if you do have any of these markers, it's as if your soul is trying to get your attention so that your special talent is lived. Gift markers appear as either a six-pointed star or line, whether straight or curved, on specific areas of your palms.

Here's a list of select markings, with their location on your hands and what they mean.

Gift Marker	Marker Location	Gift Meaning
Star of Jupiter	Under index finger on palm	The Super Achiever
Star of Saturn	Under middle finger on palm	The Midas Touch
Star of Apollo	Under ring finger on palm	Fame and Fortune in Arts
Star of Mercury	Under pinky finger on palm	Ingenuity
Star on the Moon	Low outer palm	Flashes of Intuition
Star of Wisdom	Middle zone of inside thumb	The Seer
Star of Venus	Low inner palm	The Lover of Life
Star of Mars	Inner palm near thumb	The Warrior
Star of Pluto	Outer palm between heart/headline	The Radical Transformer
Star of Neptune	Low middle palm above wrist	The Empath
Pure Heart	Curved heart line to index finger	The Humanitarian
Lines of Genius	Vertical lines on tip of pinky	Translator of Abstract Concepts for the Masses
Medical Stigmata	Vertical lines under pinky on palm	Gifted Healer Inspired Communicator

You can look at your own hands to get a glimpse of what they're showing. It's even more powerful to get a personal reading to help you unlock your code with clarity.

Your Destiny by Design

As you've likely gleaned or reaffirmed at this point, you have a predestined design, which God created together with your own soul before you were born. You don't even have to believe in a religious God to discover this, but you do need to trust some Divine source of power greater than yourself. The great news is that you also have a lot of influence and choice over how your predestined design is shaped and directed along your life path. Remember, when you are aligned with and express your divine self, you feel more joyful and alive.

Now that you have a variety of perspectives through which to see and better understand your aspects of self, you can weave these together in a way that allows you to craft a clear soul purpose mission statement. Another way to say this is that you can piece together your purpose puzzle. I trust that if you take the time to metabolize what you've deduced about yourself through any or all of these lenses, you will have a deeper understanding of who you are and what you're here to do.

I noticed in my own journey that, while each particular system offered me deep personal insight, my most powerful discovery happened when I synthesized what all of them highlighted about me into a cohesive picture. It could not be a coincidence that each lens seemed to validate, reinforce, or compliment what the others also described about my nature and ways of being. As I already said above, my MBTI® ENFP assessment enabled me to claim my idealistic, catalyzing nature. My Numerology Life Path Five reinforced for me that a big part of my mission is to facilitate change in a free-spirited way–and live a life of adventure and play. Lo and behold, my Enthusiast Enneagram profile confirmed that similar joyful, spontaneous, and adventurous aspect of my questing self. What's more, the Capricorn astrological sun under which I was born underpins my ambitious, ever-striving drive to keep climbing and achieving.

The piece de resistance that really pulled all of that together was my Soul Purpose Hand Reading. My mix of fingerprints places me in three of the four Life Schools–Love, Peace, and Wisdom–which is somewhat unusual. Wow, my soul really took on a lot to learn and master in this lifetime–no wonder it has felt so challenging at times! The print on my left Jupiter finger points to personal power, advocacy, and leadership as my Life Purpose. This mission is further flavored by the numerous gift markers I have on both hands. These include Stars of Apollo (The Arts), Stars in the Moon (Intuition), Lines of Genius (Translator of Abstract Concepts), and Medical Stigmata (Gifted Healer/Inspired Communicator). With all that, Pamelah urged me to get out there to speak, write, teach, and create. I also have a Line of Mercury, which is a marker for a channeler and quester of spiritual wisdom. When Pamelah read this particular part of my hands, she solemnly told me that it was one of the longest and straightest Mercury lines she had seen, and that it was like I had a telephone line to God, which brought tears to my eyes. In Chapter Five, I tell you about another spiritual nudge I received about being a channel for Divine wisdom.

Here is my soul purpose mission statement, based on my synthesis of my nature through each of the lenses presented above:

I am an intuitive change agent, and spiritual channel here to champion spirit-centered leadership, personal power, wellness, and living your passions. Creative expression, public speaking and writing are essential aspects to serving my soul's mission.

ACTION: New Ways to Play

∿ **Start a journal dedicated solely for Designing Your Destiny.** Make an intention to write in it every day, for at least the next thirty days, about your self from any or all of the perspectives presented here and beyond. Use different colored pencils, pens, or markers to highlight the various aspects that you discover.

∿ **Study your hands.** See if you can determine your fingerprint types on each finger and thumb to identify your Life School, Purpose, and Lesson. Also look for any gift markers you may have. Better yet, I encourage you to visit my website to schedule a professional reading so I can give you a clear identification and deeper understanding of your soul purpose through this lens.

∿ **Piece together your purpose puzzle**. First, I suggest that you take the assessment tests for the MBTI® and the Enneagram located on the related websites listed in the Endnotes. You can also calculate your Numerology Life Path yourself. Next, carve out some time to review your journal writing and browse my profile type descriptions in each of the personality systems again, along with your hand reading. Gather all this information together in your journal. Then, write down the names and tagline descriptions of each profile type within which you fall. Write your soul purpose mission statement by combining these together in any way that feels most true for you. Sign and date this, and read it out loud.

CHAPTER TWO

PAINT A PICTURE OF
YOUR PASSIONS AND
YOUR DREAM LIFE

Every great dream begins with a dreamer. Always remember,
you have within you the strength, the patience, and the passion
to reach for the stars to change the world.

~ Harriet Tubman

What do you love? What does your heart desire? What is your dream? Believe it or not, there are so many people in this world who really can't answer these questions, especially if you've lost your connection to your soul, or you've been operating on autopilot like I described in the first chapter. This question may draw a blank for you if you were raised in a family system in which you were taught to focus on the needs of others rather than yourself, or you were not encouraged to imagine and identify what it is that you like or love or are passionate about.

If that's true for you, don't feel bad. Passion is kind of an intangible thing and not that easy to pin down. It's like trying to value the goodwill of a company; goodwill is not a physical asset and represents the less visible aspects that contributed to the lifeblood and value of the business. Your passion contributes to *your* lifeblood. That's why being connected with your deep desires is so crucial to living with purpose.

For many people, the word passion has a romantic love connotation. Of course, romance and love are essential for a satisfying life. Yet, I am talking about a broader aspect of passion, the kind that can not only excite you, but also fuel your fervent pursuit of your soul's mission.

According to Merriam-Webster's dictionary, passion is a strong feeling of enthusiasm or excitement for something or about doing something. Perhaps you get excited about preparing and cooking a delicious meal, where I may be less than enthusiastic about that (even though I am Italian, so this baffles many people who know me). I am thrilled about visiting and exploring a new place I've never seen and writing about it, while my life partner is eager to capture beautiful images of that location.

Zeal is another aspect of passion that is more about action. When you feel zealous about something, like a cause or goal you care deeply about, it generates drive in pursuit of it. The energy, when engaged, can actually generate a higher vibrational tingling sensation somewhere in your body. You also want to share it with others. You almost can't stop yourself from doing this because you're so ardent about it. Passion and zeal are fire element energies.

When is the last time you felt your inner fire? Whether it's been a long time or recently, can you conjure up that memory in your mind's eye and recall the feeling it generated in your body? What was it that you felt passionate or zealous about? If you already know of one thing or activity that you love, then at least you have a start in creating your pleasure palette. Just as an artist paints from a palette with all the spectrum of colors, you can fill your pleasure palette with each of your passions as you discover or rediscover them, so that you can paint your life with more vibrancy and literally live full spectrum.

If you have a hard time identifying your desires, sometimes it helps to start by thinking of those things or activities that are prevalent in your life that you really dislike. Let's call it your discontent. Obviously, we all have to do some things in life or at work that we don't like sometimes; however, when those things are a chronic and consistent presence, they will drag down your energy and spirit. So it is important to identify them.

Speaking of discontent, let me paint a more vivid picture of my worst state of displeasure to add more color to the story that I shared in the opening of this book. First, I want to remind you of my soul purpose mission statement, created after I pieced together my own purpose puzzle to align with my true essence:

I am an intuitive change agent, and spiritual channel here to champion and inspire spirit-centered personal power and leadership, wellness, and living your passions. Creative expression, public speaking, and writing are essential aspects to serving my soul's mission.

Now, let's flash back to my days as a business and financial professional in the independent audit practice of the international accounting and consulting firm where I began my career straight out of undergraduate school with my Bachelor's Degree in Accountancy and my license as a CPA. Accounting and independent auditing of a company's financial statements involve lots of rules, regulations, and generally accepted standards and principles with which to comply. On top of that, publicly traded companies are also required to conform to the reporting requirements of the Securities and Exchange Commission, which are elaborate and complex. Compliance with regulations does not equal freedom of expression.

I'm sure you get the gist of why someone with the soul purpose written above may eventually feel tortured and boxed in serving this function as her livelihood. As my Capricorn goat self, that career path was satisfying to the part of me that strives for achievement and climbing to the top. It also allowed me to use my lines of genius gift for synthesizing complicated information and making sense of it for others. My extroverted, freedom-seeking, enthusiast self appreciated the ability to have many different clients and project teams to manage at the same time. However, my creative expression and strong spiritual aspects were not being used. And then there was the compliance stuff. In hindsight, I realized that my thoughts had become flooded eventually with the statement, *If I have to do this one more day, I'm going to die.* I literally felt like I was dying. It didn't matter how much money I was earning. Money is not the sole measure of prosperity, especially when your soul is stifled. And no amount of money is worth dying over.

Free Your Creative Spirit

What part of your life or livelihood feels most stifling to your soul right now? Are there aspects of it that do feel satisfying to you, even if there are many others that dull you down? What gifts do you have that you are able to express in your life, and which ones are you not using enough to feel happy? When you reflect on these questions, you can begin to get a clearer picture of what you love and what you would really rather live without. This can be a starting point for you to identify your passions.

Magazines and books with colorful pictures are an easy way to recapture ideas of what you love. When is the last time you allowed yourself the leisure of flipping through some magazines just for the pure pleasure of immersing in some of the images and words in them? If you're an active go-getter, you may not do this very often, because it might feel like you're "wasting time." Perhaps the next time you do so, make an intention to notice pictures that perk you up. You can take it a step further. Go to a store that sells magazines, buy a handful that spark your interest, and then take the time to look at them. Notice what topics you were drawn to.

Another potent way to uncover your passions is to reflect back on your childhood. You have an inner child version still within, and if you can tap that youth spirit, you may strike passion gold. If you think back to that time in your life when you were a carefree kid, can you recall any memories that conjure up a long-forgotten passion? Talk to your parents or other family members about your childhood years to add more color to your own emerging picture. Older people usually love talking about the good ol' days. Pull out some old photos from that time of your life to crystallize your visual memories even more.

My own childhood memories became a rich source of my buried passions. After my marriage suddenly crumbled down like a house of cards, I began to recapture earlier memories; and while some were painful, there were others that were gems. One of the most significant positive recollections for me was that, when I was a very young girl, my mother often sang songs with me and to me. We had many music rituals together that I loved and still cherish. I remembered how I loved music and to sing! This aspect of my childhood was one of many golden nuggets within some black rocks. Soon enough, it was time for me to stop sobbing and wake up to discover more of what I really loved.

Within months, I had a divinely inspired idea to allow myself to take some time off from work and my regular life. I embarked on a three-month sabbatical from this job to travel to my ancestral Italy, which went a long way to cure my blues, and, as it turns out, also to further spark my passion fire. This was an amazing gift to my workaholic self; and looking back, I still marvel that I did this. The trip and this time away were magical and pivotal in freeing my creative spirit.

I had never been to Europe, and it was liberating to leave my business suits behind and make this sojourn with simply my spirit and a backpack. The people in Italy are passionate and open, and just being around them began to heal my grief and fill me with joy. Their leisurely and fun-loving ways epitomize the opposite of the fast-paced rat race I left back home and I almost had no choice but to slow down, relax and immerse in good food, beautiful sites, and music. It didn't hurt that lots of handsome Italian men chased after me on their Vespas whistling and calling out "Ciao bella"!

Along the way, I had the opportunity to attend my first opera. When my childhood girlfriend, who was travelling with me, and I made our way to Verona, we found out that Aida was playing there at the ancient, open-air Roman amphitheater La Arena, and we scored tickets from our albergho to go see it.

Later that evening, there we sat on the stone stadium benches that seemed to vibrate with the energy of historic events that had taken place over the ages, excited for this grand opera to begin. Something about this moment felt momentous for me. The night sky was lit up with multitudes of stars that shined on the stage. As the story unfolded, the Egyptian army defeated the Ethiopians and began its triumphal march back home. When Verdi's powerful and lyrical music resounded this victory song, it filled the crisp air and resonated within me. I remembered then that I could triumph over anything.

When I returned to work, through serendipity, my office needed to assign a manager to handle its local performing arts organization clients when the person who had done so left the firm. Fresh from my Italy experience, I jumped at this chance, even though, from a career positioning perspective, it seemed crazy because nonprofit clients are not as technically demanding for a senior manager to handle. When I began to get to know the opera company client and visited their office, I immediately felt more alive once again! Beautiful music infused the space and me. The people were warm, artsy and inviting, and they even had a grand piano there.

Sensing my enthusiasm for what they were about, and also noticing I was not the stereotypical CPA, they invited me to be a supernumerary (extra) in one of their season's opera productions, La Bohéme. The experience of being immersed in the live staging rehearsals complete with costuming and characters further fueled my feeling of aliveness. I felt happy. I was in my element. I realized this aspect of my self had been missing for too long. I am a songbird and I love to sing–and to be on stage. I shared details about my participation in La Bohéme with everyone and anyone who would listen and invited them to attend any of the performances. I was lit up. Little did I know then that I have Star of Apollo gift markers on both of my hands, which mean that public recognition in the arts is a significant contributor to serving my soul mission. It is no wonder that I felt so lit up. Also look for any gift markers you may have.

Unfortunately, I still had to show up at work to manage teams of professionals to complete financial consulting projects and independent audits of companies' financial statements, which did not light up my spirit. While there are many styles of management, at a base level in this environment, it was about controlling or at least directing processes and people with a focus on ensuring that things were measuring up in agreement with rules and standards. Compared to the expansive and magical energy of music and creative expression, these activities felt constricting. As I talked about above, simply based on my essential nature, it should be understandable how this dragged down my energy.

Passion is energy. Passion is a driving force that further sparks your inner fire and gets it moving. Your inner fire, or what some call Chi, is your soul surging through your body and keeping it awake. That's why you can feel so alive when you're connected to and engaged with what you feel passionate about, because your Chi is flowing and vibrating at a higher level. When you've either lost connection to your passion or you never learned to identify what you love to begin with, your life force energy eventually slows down and can literally become stuck. That's when you may feel lethargic or depressed, or get sick, like I did.

When you are connected with or doing something that you are most passionate about, you are willing to go all out for it. Your whole body, mind, and spirit are involved; and you may even lose all sense of time and space because you are so immersed in the joy of the moments and in the ultimate outcome that you really want.

I happen to feel that way about my Italian ancestry, even more so after my passion quest to Italy; and when I discovered I might be able to obtain Italian citizenship alongside my U.S. citizenship, I went after it full steam ahead. It was a complicated and lengthy process involving a lot of research and paperwork. I needed to prove that my Italian-born ancestor who emigrated—in this case, my great-grandfather—was still a citizen of Italy when his American-born son, my grandfather, came along. This key factor is what allows for the right of citizenship to flow down the bloodline to me. The Italians call this form of citizenship *jure sanguinis*, or by the right of the blood.

To document this proof, I needed to obtain vital records—certified birth, death, and marriage certificates—for my great-grandfather and great-grandmother by tracking down these documents in Italy, and then to gather the same records for every one of his American-born descendants in my blood line.

The most difficult part of this process was to show evidence that he never naturalized after arriving in the U.S. and was, in fact, still an Italian citizen. It's not easy to prove a negative, but I found a way.

After getting all this information together, which took me over a year, I had to translate all the documents to Italian and then present my case in person to my local consulate office in San Francisco. Once they warmly welcomed me inside, a handsome Italian man offered me some delicious pastries while a woman reviewed my file, complimenting me on how well-organized it was. It didn't take long before she announced, "Complimenti!" which means congratulations, and approved my case with celebratory gusto. My primary patriotic allegiance is still to this great country where I was born, yet I'm thrilled that I am now a dual citizen of the United States and Italy.

All of that paperwork and compliance was worth it because I was passionate about the ultimate goal. I was so on fire with this opportunity that nothing would stop me from getting it done. I also really had fun discovering the information, so I was completely immersed in it when I worked on it. I shared what I was doing with just about everyone I knew and met. There are an untold number of Italian-American strangers out there that I've inspired to pursue this dual-citizenship opportunity themselves because I shared my passion.

My initial passion discoveries were just what I needed to further spark my fire and begin to paint a picture of my dream life that essentially includes music, travel, and much more. My vision was emerging. Now, let's further develop your vision.

Color Your Vision

Do you remember that moment in the movie *The Wizard of Oz* when Dorothy tentatively opened the door of her Kansas house after a tornado had whisked it away from a monochrome landscape, over the rainbow, and dropped it down in the Land of Oz? The movie screen went from flat black and white to full spectrum color. This magical moment when everything seemed to come to life made an impression on me as a child and as an adult. That's what can happen to your life when you add more color to it–figuratively and literally. Even merely adding color to your play space will make a difference in the vibrancy of your life.

Colors are simply varying qualities of light. In fact, we need light in order to be able to see colors. While color preferences and the meanings associated with them are personal, there are established connotations for the basic colors of the rainbow.

Color	Association
Red	Presence, Power, Passion
Orange	Play, Enthusiasm, Creativity
Yellow	Joy, Intellect, Personal Power
Green	Development, Health, Freshness
Blue/Indigo	Perception, Faith, Loyalty
Violet/Purple	Spirituality, Luxury, Royalty

What colors tend to attract you? How do you feel when you surround yourself and the space around you with those colors? Now that you've discovered more about your soul purpose and written your mission statement, consider the colors that may enhance your excitement about serving it. Add these colors to your pleasure palette with decorative items in your space such as candles, clothing, artwork, and any other way you imagine will spark your passion further through color.

When I practiced expressive arts therapy, I often used a collection of colored scarves as tools to help clients identify their feelings. Sometimes when a person feels down or depressed, the world may tend to look and feel black and white, or a little grey. So I also used this device as a metaphor to teach clients that, even when their life feels dull, a full spectrum of color is available to them and they can experience brightness again. Nearly all of those clients loved these colored scarves and would often drape one or more over their necks throughout the session. These scarves still brighten my office today.

Speaking of black and white, I know a woman whose entire wardrobe consisted of mostly black-colored clothing for a long period of time in her life. Eventually, she began to incorporate some colors into her repertoire, and I noticed that she came more alive and in her element by doing so. If you happen to love black, there's nothing wrong with that! I'm merely suggesting that adding color to your self and your surroundings will expand your vision of possibilities.

. . . .

Discover Your Dream

When you've filled in enough of your pleasure palette, you can use this to paint a picture of your dream life and livelihood. The picture can become a blueprint, a visual rendering, for building and co-creating this life into reality together with the Divine. And, that blueprint, along with some specific ways to shift your thinking and imagining, can take you from pure possibility to a new playground for your dream life.

The first key is to engage your imagination, which is one of the six mental faculties you possess. In addition to imagination, you also have the capacities of perception, reason, memory, will, and intuition, all of which are powerful tools you were given that sets you and every human being apart from animals! Imagination is a miraculous function—it is the language of the soul and your connection to all that is. When you imagine, you access a wealth of symbols, archetypes, metaphors, and pictures—and these are what really help you design a clear picture that can be brought to life. As Mary Morrissey teaches in The *DreamBuilder Program*, when you can see yourself as the architect of your own life rather than as the victim of circumstance, then you can begin to build your dream—one that is fueled by your passion, your persistence, and a belief in yourself that you are really worthy of having this dream.[16] An architect can't build your dream home without a blueprint, and the universe can't help you build your dream life without a vibrant vision.

In *Dream*Building, you are imagining the life you love in all of its core realms. These realms include your health and wellness, your relationships, your livelihood, and your financial freedom. When I talk about your financial freedom, I am talking about what you desire to do with your time and money.

Another *Dream*Building key to empower your visioning exercises is to imagine your dream elements as if you already have them in the present and exude appreciation that they have come to pass. I talk more about presence as one of the Seven Sacred Flames in Chapter Six. There really is no time but the present, so to live in it is a way to transform fear, doubt, or disbelief into a manifesting power that is catalyzed by thoughts and emotions. If you use language in present rather than future tense, and also infuse it with gratitude, you add an exponential energy boost to the vibration that is spinning your thoughts to your material world. One way to do this is to thank the Divine for bringing an aspect of your dream to you. You might think or say something like, "Thank you universe. I am so happy and grateful now that I'm finally dipping my feet into the turquoise waters of the Mediterranean Sea!" Gratitude has the same powerful affect on your vision as it does on how you feel in your everyday life. When you look for the blessings, everything looks much brighter and you feel better because you're raising your vibrational level—a critical component to manifesting your desires into reality.

Finally, you need to get very specific about the components of your dream. In order to get what you want, you need to be clear about what it looks, sounds, smells, feels, and tastes like. The more distinct and sharp the picture, the more the universe will be able to bring opportunities to you that you can make manifest. If you would love a new home, then instead of simply saying, "I'm so happy I'm living in my new home," you need to envision where it's located and what it looks like in visual specifics room by room. If you want to travel more, you need to specify where you want to visit, when, and how often. You get the picture.

ACTION: New Ways to Play

∿ **Create your pleasure palette.** Put together a tangible panel, like an artist's palette, with visual icons of your passions as you've uncovered or discovered them. You can also write these down in your Destiny journal. Choose one of your passions that you have been missing in your life and make an intention to reactivate it in some way over the next thirty days. If you're passionate about playing golf and have not done so, go play golf.

∿ **Create a life vision statement.** Set aside some focused time, away from all your to-do's, to let your imagination take over your thoughts and visualize yourself living your dream life–your health, your relationships, your vocation, and your freedom with money. You may start with a meditation or some inspiring music. Then write a narrative of whatever comes to your mind no matter how different or impossible it may appear than your current conditions. Make it real by using descriptive and present tense language, infused with gratitude. For example, write I am so grateful that I

_____. Sign and date it, and read it out loud every day.

~ **Create your vision board**. Use your magazines to tear out images and words that not only represent your passions, but may also depict aspects of your life vision statement. Place the images onto a poster or foam board in any way you want. You can certainly also add your own elements to it with paint or markers. You might like to organize your board into quadrants representing the areas of your life, or create one vision board dedicated solely to one realm you want to focus on first. Sign and date your vision board, and place it somewhere where you can easily see it every day.

CHAPTER 3

PRAISE YOUR PERSONAL POWER

There are powers inside of you which, if you could discover and use, would make of you everything you ever dreamed or imagined you could become.

~ Orison S. Marden

Your self-esteem, self-confidence, strong will to become and perform what you are passionate about and have been called to do is enabled by having a solid connection to your personal power. When it is strong and balanced, it's almost as if you have warrior energy that can conquer anything you set out for. If it's dulled down–which can happen even if you look successful, and you're still performing daily life and livelihood functions–you may doubt some aspects of your ability, have difficulty making decisions, or even have trouble managing anger. Praising your personal power is an impressive way to shore up your conquering spirit.

When you praise someone, you might write, say, or even sing your approval or admiration of him or her. Does this form of expression come naturally to you? It's usually easy for most of you to express accolades about and directly to another person. You can probably think of many traits, skills, accomplishments, and even natural talents of friends, family members, or people you work with more than you might ponder your own brilliant points.

Have you thought about expressing praise for yourself, directly to yourself? I know some people who do like to look themselves straight in the mirror and affirm their own character traits; however, most people I know cringe at the idea of even looking in the mirror much less stating positive messages to themselves while doing so.

Why should you even think of doing so at all? When you praise someone else, it builds up his self-esteem and confidence. Your recognition of that person, especially if he respects you, is a huge validation from an outside source that makes him feel unique, special, or even capable in the world. I remember the look on my precious nephew's face when I most recently praised his traits which I recognized and appreciated–particularly his natural talent for negotiating that he's exhibited since he was about two years old, much to my sister's frustration! He was glowing. Try to recall the last time someone commended you, and remember how you felt. To praise is to honor, lift up, and glorify, just as some of you may do for God.

If you really are a spark of the Divine, and your soul chose a life purpose and mission before you were born, along with the gifts and talents you possess to serve that purpose, then who are you NOT to praise your self? You deserve this just by the fact that you were born and that you're breathing. It is important for you to recognize all the qualities of your self, soul, and spirit as a way to claim your personal power. This is who you are, and therein lays your inner authority and your will to serve your soul mission. Increase your glowing factor!

I AM

Since you've already begun to piece together your purpose puzzle, you have a great start on your list of the essential qualities that make you who you are at your core. This is your "I AM." There are many spiritual teachers and authors who have written or talked about the concept of I AM. My own meaning and understanding of this powerful identifying language comes from the Bible.

When God appeared and spoke to Moses in the burning bush in the Exodus, and Moses asked him who he was, God told Moses, "I AM THAT I AM," and went on to elaborate that he was the God of Moses' fathers and this was his name forever. God revealed himself, simply using his most essential nature as his name, to the people of Israel through Moses.

Jesus Christ proclaimed many mighty I AM statements throughout his ministry as told in the New Testament of the Bible. These assertions served to not only teach through symbolism, but to show us how to own our personal identity.

Jesus did not just tell the disciples about what he was going to do or what was going to happen. He used language that claimed those happenings as aspects of who he was. For example, instead of just telling them that he was going to get crucified and then rise from the dead on the third day, he announced, "I am the resurrection and the life."

During my yearlong hospitalized trial through leukemia, one of my practices was to praise Jesus out loud in a litany of prayer for all of his I AM essences. I actually translated his I AM statements into You Are, the way you would talk to someone you were giving praise to. So I would recite, "Praise you, Jesus,

> You are the way, the truth and the life.
> You are the light of the world.
> You are the bread of life.
> You are the gate.
> You are the living water.
> You are the good shepherd.
> You are the true vine. . . ."

I added more aspects of Jesus to this prayer litany beyond what the Bible says Jesus claimed in his I AM statements. Praise you Jesus, you are my healing and wholeness; by your wounds, I am healed, and more. I know that doing this elevated my vibrational level, which further stimulated my healing. I also felt good just saying these things. And since I know that I am one with God and one with Jesus, I also began to praise myself with the same kind of prayer litany, using my own I AM statements.

I am Lauren Marie Perotti.

I am a spark of the Divine.

I am Chiara.

I am a lightworker.

I am a songbird.

I am an intuitive change agent.

I am a champion for creative expression, passion, and purpose. . . .

You get the idea. I felt so energized and empowered—and even enlightened—by doing this practice then, and I still do this now as a key part of my spiritual practice.

Your name is part of your identity and your essential nature. When you introduce yourself to another person, you usually say, "Hi, I am [your name]," to identify yourself. Whenever you say the words I AM, you are distinguishing yourself. So the labels or words you connect with or attach to your individual I AM statements are important. Do you ever catch yourself saying things like, "I am so bored," or any number of other negative ways you may currently feel? There may even be occasions when you believe you screwed something up and may inadvertently say something like, "I am so stupid," or a similar self-sabotaging sentiment. When you do so, you are claiming that as part of who you are. Instead, why not name and claim your essential nature? There are actually some comprehensive I AM study programs available, and you can pursue those at any point in your journey. No matter how deep you go with this, it will be empowering for you to write down and speak aloud your I AMs.

Your core values

Stand up for what you believe in! This is another way to bolster your personal power. Are you clear about what those beliefs or values are? A business or nonprofit organization will usually define its top values in alignment with its mission statement. Yet, when is the last time you reflected on the guiding ideals or principles you hold to be most important for your personal or family life, or livelihood?

Sometimes, the particular values you feel most strongly about may change over time as you go through the different phases and ages of your life. Now that you are embarking on a period of discovery and design of your next destined dream life and livelihood, it's a perfect time to take stock of your core values so that you can align your purpose and life direction with them.

Most people feel empowered and more satisfied with their life when what they're doing is congruent with their strongest beliefs. One way you can start to create a conscious list of your fundamental values is to reflect on the times when you feel happy and in harmony with the situation and people around you and determine what factors influenced your feeling of congruence. You could also think of situations in which you regularly feel off balance somehow. For example, if you realize that you feel alive and uplifted when you collaborate with others on a project, you might list Teamwork as a possible core value. Similarly, you might have the same insight if you mostly work alone and realize this is seriously contributing to your unhappiness.

You may already know what you believe in, yet still accept conditions that conflict with those beliefs. Sometimes that stems from a lack of belief in your own deservingness to have good in your life–even if you are highly capable in most arenas. Do you find yourself bending over backwards, rearranging your own emotional state or values, or doing for others at your own expense? If you have this telltale marker on your heart line on one or both of your hands–and I can tell you if you do by looking at your palms for less than a minute–you might be even more susceptible to doing this. But, the clearer you are about your highest values, the better equipped you are to speak your truth in relationships and situations. When you do so, you further shore up your power.

Here is a list of some common values to help guide your process. You can start by eliminating those with which you do not resonate at all. Then, keep working through the list to rank those that are remaining until you have identified your top five values by asking yourself if that value is more important than each one remaining, and so on. It may seem simple enough, but sometimes it is challenging to prioritize one over another.

A LIST OF CORE VALUES

Acceptance	Accountability	Action	Adventure	Authenticity
Balance	Beauty	Boundaries	Celebration	Change
Choice	Clarity	Commitment	Communication	Community
Compassion	Confidence	Congruency	Connection	Consciousness
Consistency	Conviction	Cooperation	Courage	Creativity
Decisiveness	Dedication	Dependability	Determination	Development
Devotion	Diligence	Diplomacy	Discipline	Discovery
Diversity	Drive	Education	Efficiency	Empathy
Encouragement	Endurance	Enlightenment	Expertise	Expressiveness
Evolution	Faith	Flexibility	Flow	Focus
Forgiveness	Freedom	Fun	Generosity	Giving
Gratitude	Harmony	Happiness	Health	Holiness
Honesty	Hope	Humor	Idealism	Imagination
Impact	Independence	Integrity	Intention	Joy
Knowledge	Leadership	Learning	Love	Loyalty
Majesty	Mastery	Mindfulness	Motivation	Neatness

Openness	Optimism	Organization	Originality	Passion
Peace	Perseverance	Philanthropy	Planning	Playfulness
Professionalism	Prosperity	Purpose	Reason	Recreation
Resilience	Respect	Responsibility	Sacredness	Sacrifice
Service	Spirituality	Strength	Success	Synergy
Teamwork	Trust	Truth	Understanding	Unity
Valor	Wealth	Wisdom	Wonder	Zeal

Once you have your list, you can ask yourself some questions. Are your top five core values being expressed in your life now? Which areas of your life are not aligned with any or all of your values? Sometimes, if there is a job or relationship or activity that you are involved in that so entirely conflicts with your core values, you may need to release or disengage from it. If you are not able to abandon the situation, is there a way that you can consciously bring your values to it?

Talents and Skills

When is the last time you took an inventory of your talents and skill set? You can probably just pull out your last resume to remind yourself of the particular skills that make you good at performing your job function and how great you really are. That may seem as if it's egotistical, but confidently acknowledging your strengths is a sign of mental health, and it is empowering.

You have a broader range of talents you perform or can express and apply in all the realms of your life, some of which may have become so hidden that you've forgotten that you even possess them. That's why I also decided to include yet another chart to help stimulate your identification of those gifts you want to unleash. Once you do, you'll be even more aware of these parts of you, and you can praise those too.

Skills, Talents and Gifts

Accounting	Acting	Advising	Advocating	Analyzing
Architecture	Artistry	Astrology	Astronomy	Assembling
Baking	Balancing	Beautifying	Brainstorming	Budgeting
Building	Camping	Caretaking	Carpentry	Categorizing
Clairvoyance	Coaching	Collaborating	Comedy	Communicating
Computers	Conceptualizing	Consulting	Cooking	Creativity
Dancing	Decision-making	Decluttering	Decorating	Demonstrating
Designing	Doctoring	Drawing	Encouraging	Entertaining
Entrepreneurism	Events	Family	Farming	Fashion
Filmmaking	Finance	Fishing	Fitness	Fundraising
Gardening	Goal-setting	Healing	Ideas	Improvisation
Inspiration	Interviewing	Intuition	Inventing	Languages
Leadership	Listening	Magic	Managing	Marketing
Mediating	Missions	Music	Naturopathy	Negotiating
Networking	Nursing	Optimizing	Organizing	Painting
Parenting	Persuasion	Photography	Planning	Playing an Instrument

Pottery	Prophecy	Public Speaking	Recruiting	Research
Retreats	Resolving Conflicts	Sculpting	Selling	Singing
Social Media	Sports	Storytelling	Strategizing	Synthesizing
Talent Searching	Teambuilding	Therapy	Training	Videography
Visioning	Wilderness	Workshops	Writing	Youth Development

Personal Responsibility

When you give your power away to other people as a regular habit of being, you tend to see yourself as a powerless, victim of life. You blame other people, society, or the world for your inability to discover or activate your desires. But when you own the responsibility for your happiness, you boost your personal power immeasurably. Of course, when you are a young child, you don't have as many choices. It is important to recognize conditions from the past that were wounding and may have contributed to your soul's suppression. It is important to be able to resolve these feelings as an adult and accept your responsibility for your own life path. Let go of feeling like a victim—let God and move on.

At a certain point in my awakening, personal development journey, I finally had a big aha moment, one of many of course. I realized I was responsible for my own happiness. What a concept! I understood that if I continued to attach my happiness and sense of meaning and purpose to outside conditions that could come or go or change at the drop of a hat, I would never realize consistent happiness and joy. The same was true about believing something that might never change needed to change in order for me to feel happy. When I placed my focus outwardly like this, I was giving away my personal power. I could only have this realization once I became conscious that this was actually a way of being and that there was another way to think about this. I have a choice. Awareness is the first key, as I've said.

The more I accepted the truth that I could be happy regardless of any outside conditions, which I finally really did on a deep level during my leukemia battle, the more empowered I felt to create my own happiness and a life and livelihood that brings me joy, playfulness, passion, adventure, and purpose.

It's also crucial for you to understand that you are NOT responsible for anyone else's happiness. There is a difference between caring about another person and their happiness, and somehow taking on the responsibility for it. Another person might try to make you feel responsible for his or her happiness, consciously, or unconsciously. You are not responsible for anyone else's happiness or life satisfaction. You ARE responsible for your own happiness and fulfillment, and you are responsible for fulfilling your soul's life mission.

Your Life Stories and Personal Narrative

Your ability to develop a strong connection to your personal power can be influenced by the stories you tell yourself or that were told to you, sometimes at a young age. Do you remember any tales you were told in the past that you still carry with you? If so, how do they influence your sense of self-confidence?

There were many rich stories from my family history that were relayed by the older generations—grandparents, great grandparents, great aunts and uncles, and more. I heard these because I was around them a lot growing up. In fact, still today, whenever I hear Dean Martin crooning, "That's Amore," it conjures up old images–almost like black-and-white Polaroids of scenes from my Italian family upbringing. Our Italian traditions included weekly gatherings at my grandparents' home to eat, drink, play cards and other games, tell stories, and sing. All of my cousins, aunts, and uncles, and even great-grandparents, would be there. I can picture my uncle playing his accordion while my dad and others sang along, my grandma making sauce and meatballs in the steamy kitchen, and a house full of laughter, music, smoke, and alcohol, with people cursing and loving, all mixed together into some kind of dramatic storytelling sonata.

My great-grandmother–my Dad's paternal grandmother– often told me the story of how she left Italy in 1910 when she was only about seventeen and hopped aboard a transatlantic boat by herself to come to America. Sure, her father and brother had already come over, so it wasn't quite as daunting an endeavor as it may have been had she not known a soul here. But, she was so avid to forge a new life path that she somehow edged in front of her older sister, whose turn it was to come next, and she didn't wait for her dad to return to Italy to accompany her. Something tells me she would have embarked on this journey even if she had been on her own in this vast country of opportunity. That kind of pioneering resolve inspired my can-do spirit.

Then there was a particular story my mother used to tell me when I was a little girl. During the arduous task of brushing my long, thick mane of hair every morning, she would try to quell my impatience and fidgeting–and make it fun instead–by singing songs and telling stories, encouraging me to chime in. When I invariably started to wiggle and tell her to hurry, she'd first tell me to just stay still a little more. If I responded with, "I can't," she launched into the story of *The Little Engine That Could*.

This classic symbolic story written by Watty Piper is about a little blue engine that had the courage and inner power to haul a stranded train up and over a mountain. When the little engine reached the most challenging part of the journey, it kept chanting, "I think I can, I think I can . . ." all the way up that steep side of the mountain.

When my mom got to that part of the story, she urged me to chant along. When the little engine made it over the summit, it happily exclaimed, "I thought I could, I thought I could" all the way down the other side. I embodied the story; I became the Little Engine That Could. Decades later, I still carry it within me, knowing that I can do anything I think I can do–especially when I connect with a power greater than myself!

The beauty and potency of stories is that you can always create a new personal narrative for yourself and tell that one! It can be as simple as reframing an experience by the language you use or by literally focusing on a benefit rather than the problem. This is the focus of a particular form of psychotherapy called Narrative Therapy, in which the therapist helps the client co-author a new narrative about himself by focusing on skills and strengths to reshape dominant self-talk and rewrite his self-identify.

Blending Your Might and Magic

When it comes right down to it, we each have all the power we need within ourselves to be and do what we are here for. Your soul and the Divine did not co-create your purpose and mission without infusing you with all you need to fulfill it, including opportunities to develop more of what you need to grow. It's all up to you to learn the lessons you need to keep growing and walking your life path.

Each of the characters in *The Wizard of Oz* was seeking the wisdom of the Wizard to help them by giving them a quality they thought they were lacking. The Scarecrow wanted a brain; the Tin Man wanted a heart; the Lion wanted Courage and, of course, Dorothy wanted to go back home, even though she had wanted so desperately to leave.

If you've ever seen this classic movie, and I don't know many people who have not, you may recall many moments in the story's unfolding in which each of these characters displayed the very aspects of self they thought they lacked. And in the end, Dorothy found out she had the magical power all along to get home. These moments are a blending of might and magic. When you magnify your might and look for the magic in the moment, your path can be like glimmering gold.

ACTION: New Ways to Play

∿ **Praise Your Self.** Create a ritual in which you celebrate your essential self.

∿ **Claim Your "I AMs."** Write a potent litany of I AM statements that speak to your essential nature as you now know or understand it. Speak it aloud to reinforce it. Consider doing so in front of a mirror. Notice how this feels.

∿ **Name Your Core Values, Talents, and Gifts.** Create your own list or grid of your top core values along with your talents and gifts. Pay particular attention to those skills or talents that you don't tend to recognize in yourself, or that may not show up on your resume. Brainstorm ways that you can or would like to exercise those more.

PART TWO

Sustain Your Flame

Do not let your fire go out, spark by irreplaceable spark in the hopeless swamps of the not-quite, the not-yet, and the not-at-all. Do not let the hero in your soul perish in lonely frustration for the life you deserved and have never been able to reach. The world you desire can be won. It exists ... it is real ... it is possible ... it's yours.

~ Ayn Rand

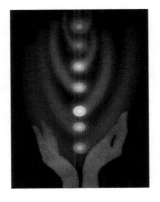

CHAPTER 4

DECLUTTER AND DESIGN
YOUR PLAY SPACE

*In every job that must be done, there is
an element of fun.*

~ Mary Poppins

I t's time to address a key aspect to manifesting a life you
love that may not sound like fun for most of you. In fact,
you may want to skip right over this and hope you can
realize transformational results anyway. But here it is: It is
absolutely essential to clear out the clutter in every area of
your life in order to make space for what you desire more of
and keep your inner fire burning.

The condition of your outer space and life affects your
inner state and vice versa. If your office or home tends to

be jumbled, then you'd be amazed at how confused or disorganized your mind can become. And when your mind is buzzing with all kinds of busy thoughts, your space may become bombarded with things that block you from realizing the results you want. Your disorder does not have to be at a level at which a friend or family member might be thinking of referring you to the television show *Hoarders* for it to be dulling down your energy and your inner fire.

The clutter that this show addresses focuses on physical things and people's houses. When I talk about clutter, I'm not only referring to stuff. I'm also talking about relationships and health, ways of thinking, unfinished business, and even your heart. I'm basically talking about taking stock of anything and everything this isn't really working for you, some of which you may have been carrying around with you for years, that may be blocking your ability to manifest new situations and things and people into your world. Releasing blocks in your life can restore the natural flow of your life force energy, increasing vitality and hope.

As with most large undertakings, the process of bringing order to your chaos can seem daunting if you think of the whole picture and all the steps that might be necessary in its entirety. Doing so is what often causes status quo and stuckness. So how can you clear your inner and outer space, and where do you begin? A good place to start is with your physical space.

Make Cleaning Up Fun

In the popular Disney movie from the '60s, *Mary Poppins*, Julie Andrews plays the musical nanny who magically shows up at the Banks home at a time when the family is in dire need of reordering every area of their lives and after many other nannies have come and gone, unable to help. Immediately after she arrives, she starts with the children's playroom, which is in obvious extreme disarray. In order to engage the help of these two precious beings, she tells them that, "In every job that must be done, there is an element of fun. When you find the fun (she snaps her fingers), the job's a game." Then she breaks into song about taking a spoonful of sugar to help the medicine go down, and soon the kids are happily cleaning up their room with a lot of fairy-tale like help. While you won't likely have birds and animals and a charmed nanny showing up to help you, you certainly can adopt a mindset to make your process fun and playful.

I'm smiling right now when I remember a time my nephew Luca was about three-years-old and his sister just a toddler. There were toys strewn all over the kitchen floor, and it was a mess. My sister called out that it was time to clean up, and, before I knew it, Luca was sweeping up with a broom three times his height singing, "Clean up, clean up, everybody do your share." Music is a great way to add fun to just about anything.

Turn on some inspiring music and state an intention to free up your space. Then, take a look around each room in your home or work or creative space. Can you make an honest assessment of how much extraneous stuff you see right out in the open? Are there piles of papers, newspapers, magazines or other items like that covering your counters or tables? Do you have a lot of trinkets cluttering your shelves? Most important, how do you feel when you're in this space? Relaxed, centered, and inspired? Anxious and scattered? Something else?

Now you can carve out how much of your space you plan to focus on for the day and what other times you can finish what's left. Then, it's helpful to create categories for items you cull through such as Trash (or shred), Donate, and Keep (and store) and have some colored post-it notes to tag things by the groupings. Now you're ready to start. You might be amazed at how different you'll feel once you start purging and organizing. If you have children, put them to play in this project.

Once you finish the more overt areas, you can dig a little deeper into the more hidden corners of your space. Do you have clothing or other items in your closets or storage bins that you have not looked at in more than a year or longer? If so, it's time to let that item go, unless it has serious sentimental value as memorabilia.

Even though I'm a fairly organized person, I used to keep lots of tchotchkes and clothing around for years. I guess I thought I needed them to remember symbolic times of my life. I've moved a lot in my life, and transferred these items with me from house to house, eventually just leaving them packed in the moving boxes where they sat in closets until the next move. There's nothing inherently wrong with keeping treasures, but at a certain point, I knew there were things I could toss to make room for the new. When I completed another purging project recently, I not only felt freed up again, but a new writing and publishing opportunity showed up for me.

I grew up in a pristinely clean and nicely decorated home. Today, I count this as one of the additional blessings of my family life, even though this used to feel like a curse based on what it was like to live this way. Back in those days, my mother, who is now a recovering clean freak, was always on herself and me and my siblings to clean our rooms, clean the bathroom, fold the clothes, wipe the kitchen counters, put the dishes in the dishwasher and on and on—not in a fun way. We were not allowed to leave anything laying around on the floor or anywhere that it might look messy.

On the flipside, I had friends whose bedrooms were strewn with clothes all over the floor and junk everywhere else, and I was amazed that this was somehow okay in their household. I didn't like the feeling of that extreme either. I intuitively knew there must be a way to strike a balance between obsessive-compulsive order and messiness. Balance is key. The blessing for me is, because of my upbringing, I know how to maintain beauty and balance, which I discovered are two of my soul's highest values.

Release or Redefine Relationships

Whether we're talking about family, friend, intimate love or life partner, work colleague, boss, or whoever you engage with on any regular basis, human relations can be the most challenging realm of life–and of course, a source of rich growth. Part of de-cluttering this area is recognizing when healing, growth, and transformation is called for in a relationship or when it is time to release that person and let him or her go, ideally, with love and light. This is not easy or for the faint of heart. It takes courage, honesty, a connection to your truth, and a commitment to both serving and living your potential to make this assessment and act on it when the time feels right.

This is a process that will require you to answer some tough questions for yourself. Does this relationship bring more blessings than challenges to your life? Are you and this person walking on the course of a complimentary vision, or do your directions seem to be diverging? Is there an imbalance in the dynamic of giving and receiving involved? You can think of more questions, but the key one is, can any of this be realigned or redefined? If you decide that this relationship can't continue in its current state, it still may be possible for you to redefine it, if you both choose to do so.

When it feels true that releasing this relationship is in your highest good, then you need to trust that it is also in that person's highest good. It couldn't work any other way. You will both be more empowered to further unfold your higher potential. And if you can also acknowledge the gifts that this person brought you, all the better. As you reflect on where you are with key relationships in your life, here is a poem written by an unknown author that can help you decide how to resolve them.

"People come into your life for a reason, a season or a lifetime.
When you figure out which one it is,
you will know what to do for each person.
When someone is in your life for a REASON,
it is usually to meet a need you have expressed.
They have come to assist you through a difficulty;
to provide you with guidance and support;
to aid you physically, emotionally or spiritually.
They may seem like a godsend, and they are.
They are there for the reason you need them to be.

Then, without any wrongdoing on your part or at an inconvenient time, this person will say or do something to bring the relationship to an end.

Sometimes they die. Sometimes they walk away.
Sometimes they act up and force you to take a stand.
What we must realize is that our need has been met, our desire fulfilled; their work is done.
The prayer you sent up has been answered and now it is time to move on.
Some people come into your life for a SEASON,

because your turn has come to share, grow or learn.
They bring you an experience of peace or make you laugh.
They may teach you something you have never done.
They usually give you an unbelievable amount of joy.
Believe it. It is real. But only for a season.

LIFETIME relationships teach you lifetime lessons;
things you must build upon in order to have a solid
emotional foundation.
Your job is to accept the lesson, love the person,
and put what you have learned to use in all other
relationships and areas of your life.
It is said that love is blind but friendship is clairvoyant."[17]

Remiss Resentments that Weigh You Down

Just as unhealthy relationships may hold you back, if you
are still holding on to any feelings of resentment, anger, or
guilt toward another person or yourself, it's as if you are
carrying around heavy weights that will bog you down and
keep you stuck. It's a subtler form of clutter. Your willingness
to identify any of these burdens and discard them is another
step that will free you to manifest your dream. Imagine how
much lighter you'd feel if you tossed away a backpack full
of bricks you'd been hauling around on your back year after
year? These bricks can be anything from old childhood hurts
to a friend's betrayal to something your spouse said or did
to you and more.

I had spent many years and ways trying to resolve hurts I had with my mother. Even though I had made a lot of progress about those aspects of our relationship that had wounded me, I still felt blocked because I couldn't get past how I felt with her in the present. The crux was that I wanted her to be different with me than she was, something which I had no control over changing or fixing. I actually knew this in my head, but my heart was still holding on to this resentment, and I know this was a factor that contributed to my getting leukemia.

When I was at the beginning of that trial, something in me knew that finally reconciling with and forgiving my mother was critical to my healing from this dis-ease. But I had already tried so hard and hadn't been able to release it, so how could this happen? I became entirely ready and willing for God, through the power of the Holy Spirit, to free me from this burden that was keeping me blocked and had contributed to my getting this life-threatening illness. I was done with it. I was not going to let this kill me. So I asked God to do it. As the Bible says in Matthew 7:7, "Ask, and it shall be given you; seek, and ye shall find; knock, and it shall be opened unto you." The door was opened.

The very next day, a veil was lifted. I literally saw my mother in a whole new light as her essential spiritual self. It was that immediate and miraculous! I felt immense love for her and wanted her to be freed from whatever hurts and wounds might still be blocking her from feeling her own happiness and joy. It was almost as if the lifting of that un-forgiveness washed away my leukemia–it removed a block to allow the flow of my life force energy! To forgive is remiss, and being in remission from a disease is one way of saying that it is no longer there. Forgiving my mother not only helped me heal physically, it freed me up to design my life space in a new more playful way.

Don't forget to put yourself on the top of your list of people to forgive. Many of us could hold ourselves hostage in some way by regretting our own past mistakes or decisions that, in hindsight, may not have seemed the best. If that's true for you, try to find a way to trust that you did the best you could with where you were at the time, and use it as a lesson learned so you can make different choices going forward. For example, I know a woman who still tends to beat herself up sometimes about the way she interacted with her young adult son the last time she saw him before he died tragically of a drug overdose. I've coached her to trust that she did the best she could in that moment, to remember all the wonderful ways she did show her love for him, and to know has he forgiven her.

You may believe that to forgive someone means that you're making an unacceptable act that he or she did okay. Forgiveness has nothing to do with the other person. When you hang onto resentments and hurts, you are actually keeping yourself in your own prison. Once you become aware of and acknowledge those burdens that are keeping you locked up, forgiveness is a key that can unlock that prison door to your vision-driven dream.

Reorient Your Thinking

Let's admit it—even the most confident of us have at least some limiting beliefs or perceptions about ourselves that create doubt about possibilities. When you think about what's possible for your life, do you base it on your current conditions, or life circumstances? If so, you are not alone. People tend to think about what is achievable based on what they have right now and can't see a new option for the future. The problem is that most of your current conditions are limiting when you view them through your immediate five senses and your thinking. Limiting beliefs are like mental muck—they stop you from designing your dream play space.

I can't tell you how many times I have heard a friend, family member or even a client exclaim that he or she **can't** do something because of a lack of time, energy, money, or some other life circumstance that would prevent it from being realistic. When you are operating from your smaller self, you tend to be driven and guided by the needs of your ego. I can't afford it; I don't have time; I have a wife and kids, mortgage, etc. It seems like valid reasoning, doesn't it? How can I change my job, even though it's killing my soul, when I have evidence right in front of me that clearly looks like I can't? So why even try, or why even contemplate going after a dream, or making a change in life, even though it will fuel my passion and aliveness?

But when you live your life from a vision-driven mindset, you are open to possibilities, which also further ignites your passion. The key to shift into vision-driven living is to learn how to reorient your thinking and engage your other mental faculties of intuition and imagination so that you can explore possibilities. I did this unconsciously when I took a luxuriously leave instead of telling myself all the reasons I couldn't do it—I can't leave work, I can't afford it, I don't speak foreign languages, . . . There was something more powerful than any limiting condition operating within me and in the universe that made this one vision possible.

You have absolutely unlimited creative capacities. Once you practice this new paradigm on one thing, eventually it becomes easier to adopt it as a natural way of thinking. And once you can change your way of thinking, you hold the power to create whatever you want to. Where our thoughts go, the energy flows. Everything that exists in material form began with a thought. You deserve to be free and design the life you are destined for. It is now time to amplify your sense of deserving and live from your vision, because that opens you up to the magnetic field that invokes the law of attraction to bring you circumstances, situations, and resources that support what you need to bring forth your dream.

Complete Unfinished Business

If you're human, then you probably have at least a handful of things you've either started to do but never finished, or actions you've intended to take but never got around to—even if it's as simple as calling someone you haven't spoken to in a long time. These incomplete projects or tasks are yet another level of clutter. Even if you're not thinking about these on a conscious level, there is a part of you that knows they're not done, and this can serve to keep you spinning or stuck. Do you know what your incompletes are, and are you ready to finally check them off your list? Completion could literally be your acknowledgment that you will never finish that project or task so you can finally check it off your mental list. When you complete your unfinished business, you'll be even more ready to unleash your genius.

Unleash Your Genius

I like to think of your genius as those brilliant parts of you that shine because they express the gifts, character traits, and honed skills that make you unique. When you express your genius, you can exponentially increase your level of success and satisfaction in business and beyond. Your genius may be blocked if your life is cluttered with activities that keep you operating primarily in lower zones of your competency.

In his book *The Big Leap*, Gay Hendricks suggests that most people operate in various zones of competence ranging from incompetence to competence, excellence, or genius. It's when you truly identify and own what falls into each of your zones and then let go of or delegate tasks that are consuming your lower zones of ability that you can free up your inner soul space and shine. When you are operating in your genius zone, your life feels more fluid and expansive because you are engaging your essential nature and gifts.[18]

Do you know where you spend your time during a typical week? If you actually take an inventory of your activities, you might be surprised by how much time you might be spending on tasks you're either not very good at or that you really abhor. This is another level of clutter than can be bogging you down. There are one hundred and sixty-eight hours in a week. If you allow for an average of eight hours of sleep every night and time to eat and take care of other bodily needs, you probably have almost ninety hours of time in your week to fill with activities. What does your time calendar look like? What is it filled with? To get a really clear picture of this, you can make a list of all the activities you engage in from the time you wake up until you go to sleep. Then, categorize each by the zone of competence in which it lies. This will help you recognize, and hopefully make a plan to let go of, those activities that are not serving your highest vision.

There may be tasks in your incompetence zone that you are simply not good at and should be handing off. Other tasks on your list may be things you like, but don't come that easily and take a lot of your energy, so doing these may deplete you even though you are capable of doing them. Hopefully, you do spend some amount of time on things at which you excel and are recognized for your efforts, even though these activities don't necessarily come entirely easily either. Finally, do you have any tasks on your list that you just can't wait to do and leave you feeling energized? Those are the things that fall into your genius zone, and the more time you spend there, the happier you will be. Now what if you were to design your ideal ways of how you spend the time of your days? I like to call this your play space.

ACTION: New Ways to Play

~o **Design Your New Space.** Celebrate your progress in purging and organizing your home, office, and/or your creative space. Envision a new way you can rearrange the space and add some inspiring elements to it.

~o **Empower Your Beliefs.** Create a list of empowering thoughts and beliefs for yourself and practice saying these.

~o **Express More of Your Genius.** After you've created your categorized list of typical daily activities, focus on those that are in your genius zone. Make a commitment to spend more time on at least one of those things for the next thirty days. If you don't have anything in that zone now, imagine what genius you could add into your life and practice doing it. It will help if you have released tasks from your less brilliant zones.

CHAPTER 5

DANCE WITH UNIVERSAL SOURCES OF ENERGY AND LIGHT

There are two ways of spreading light; to be the candle or the mirror that reflects it.

~ Edith Wharton

I don't know about you, but I've found that it's sometimes easier to start something than it is to keep it going consistently. It's like when you start a fire—at first it may blaze brightly for a little while, just like when you first ignite your purpose, passion and power. But unless you keep fueling and stoking that real fire, it begins to flicker and even burn out. That is what can happen to your inner fire if you don't sustain it consistently. The excitement wears off, supporters in your vision may fall away, old ways of thinking set back in and, before you know it, you are back on your passionless plateau, looking okay and doing the same things, but not dancing with joy.

In the past, you may have relied on other people, places, and things to provide your source of meaning, good feelings or even physical and mental energy. The challenge with this usually unconscious strategy is that those sources can be transient and inconsistent, and you may find yourself on a roller coaster of states of feeling or being when you link your happiness to that which can come and go. As a result, you may tend to control and force solutions, rather than flow to them, which can leave you feeling irritable, drained, and out of balance.

Fortunately, there are natural sources of powerful agents that are always available, and when you unite with any or all of them, you can sustain the flame of your inner life force energy. While you do so, you may be amazed at how much more alive and present you feel. These are important states of being to manifest the life you desire. When you dance, you move in a natural rhythm and sequence of steps. So my suggestion that you dance with these sources means you can get into a regularity of accessing and connecting with them. I categorize these universal sources into realms that are of a more lasting or everlasting nature.

The Realm of Chakras

The chakras are portals for receiving light from this spiral, ever-expanding Universe, including astronomical bodies and Mother Earth. These centers of energy in your subtle body help the flow of your life force through your entire being and help maintain balance among your mental, physical, and spiritual aspects of self. In Sanskrit, the word chakra means "wheel," because historical perspectives have described them as spinning wheels of light. There are many such centers according to most texts, but the seven primary chakra points and colors are most essential. Here is a simple outline for you:

෴ **Chakra 1** – The root chakra is the very foundation of your core survival (health and prosperity), trust, and family (tribe) association. Its color of light is red.

෴ **Chakra 2** – Your sacral chakra relates to pleasure, play, creativity, feelings and sensations, and being in the moment. Its color of light is orange.

෴ **Chakra 3** – The solar plexus chakra connects to self-esteem, personal power, and the will to move forward and get things done. Its color of light is yellow.

෴ **Chakra 4** – Your heart chakra is associated with love, passion, and healing. Its color of light is green.

෴ **Chakra 5** – This is the throat chakra, which activates self-expression, your ability to speak your truth, and manifest your goals and desires. Its color of light is blue.

෴ **Chakra 6** – Your brow chakra, otherwise known as the "third eye," is essential for activating perception, intuition, imagination, and "seeing" possibilities. Its color of light is indigo.

～ **Chakra 7** – Your crown chakra is the primary portal for connecting to your own spiritual nature and the greater spirit, Divine, God, or whatever you may personally call the spirit that is greater than you are. Its color of light is violet or white.

Activating your chakras is one of the most potent sources for living on purpose, and there are many ways to do so. Each of the Seven Sacred Flames, which I talk about in the next chapter, will offer a particular perspective and practice for its related chakra. Each of the Seven Sacred Flames carries a quality or principle that correlates with the particular energy and function of each chakra. As you will discover in more depth in the next chapter, each Flame can be energized and sustained by practices that incorporate connections with all the realms I talk about here.

The Realm of Unconditional Love

The Beatles sang, "Limitless undying love, which shines around me like a million suns, it calls me on and on across the universe." When it comes down to it, there is nothing more powerful than love. Pastors and priests preach of it, children naturally exude it, poets muse about it, musicians write songs and sing about it. Love changes everything. Love lifts us up where we belong. Love is the answer. Love is a many splendored thing. Love makes the world go 'round. Love is all you need. Love is alive.

I'm not only talking about romantic love, though of course this form of it does make most of us feel more alive—I know it does for me, at least most of the time! I'm not even speaking solely to particular religious, Godly ideas of love–though these notions are real, too. First and foremost, I'm talking about the very essence of love, which is a tangible energy that can be intentionally cultivated and activated. Love is the ultimate energy that sustains the universe and all that resides within it.

You can connect to this powerful, palpable source anytime and all the time to energize, empower and enlighten every aspect of your life. When you receive it, you can emanate and share it–which causes it to grow and expand. One way to do so is to make a decision to become and act unconditionally loving, which you can do more easily if you are connected to and infused with it. Imagine what an amazing ripple effect of sparkling light we can create across our world if we each decide to practice this way of living and being.

How do you know, or how can you discover, that love is a powerful source of energy and light? It is, after all, invisible to your eyes. Or is it? All forms of matter vibrate at various energetic frequencies, and love both elicits and is the highest vibrational frequency. This can be measured with today's technology such as brain scans that clearly show how regions of your brain change with differing thoughts and emotions, and even EKGs that measure the electrical frequency of your heart, which you've just read is the center of your love energy. There are also many scientists and institutes that focus on quantum physics, neuroscience, and energy medicine, and show that your thoughts and feelings–which impact your own vibrational frequency–influence how matter in the universe becomes material form. Deepak Chopra has been probably one of the most well known experts in this field for many years now; not only has he written several books on this topic, but he founded his own center in 1996 focused on the wellness of mind, body, and spirit. The purpose of my book is not to go into profound details and research on this subtopic, but to introduce the concept that many believe love is a powerful healing and manifesting energy.

I can almost literally see and definitely feel the high energy of love when I am with babies and young children–and I so enjoy being in their presence because of this; it infuses me with more light and love. Couples who are in love can exude a high energy that glows and vibrates out. People who are in deep meditation or prayer, and coming from a desire to connect with their source of love also vibrate at high frequencies. One day, I was silently engaged in this very process while in flight on an airplane; when I completed my meditation, the woman sitting next to me told me she could feel the energy pulsating around me.

Those who are clairvoyant can see auras–the field of energy we each have around our bodies–and vibrational frequency and colors associated with them. All forms of matter have an auric field of vibration. In the musical *Jesus Christ Superstar*, the rocks and stones themselves came alive and sang "Hosanna" when Jesus came to share his message of love. Of course, this is a dramatized musical movie, but it is making a point.

Many sacred texts and ascended masters have something to say about the power of nonattached love. According to the Dhammapada, one of the most widely read and best known Buddhist scriptures, Buddha said, "Hatred does not cease by hatred, but only by love; this is the eternal rule." In Judaism, the Torah commands people to love one another. And Christians believe that God so loved us that he begat Jesus to teach the world how to love one another, even our enemies. One of my favorite verses about love in the Bible is in Paul's first letter to the Corinthians, where he told them:

"Love never fails. But where there are prophecies, they will cease; where there are tongues, they will be stilled; where there is knowledge, it will pass away. For we know in part and we prophesy in part, but when completeness comes, what is in part disappears. When I was a child, I talked like a child, I thought like a child, I reasoned like a child. When I became a man, I put the ways of childhood behind me. For now we see only a reflection as in a mirror; then we shall see face to face. Now I know in part; then I shall know fully, even as I am fully known. And now these three remain: faith, hope and love. But the greatest of these is love."[19]

Though I'm talking about love here, faith and hope are also values that can shine light into any darkness you face or feel.

At the heart of all these perspectives is the commandment to love God and love others, as much as you love yourself, all of which entails an outward, giving energy that can circle back around for receiving. It was the outpouring of unconditional love onto me that ultimately healed my leukemia. I've found that when I am living in unconditional love and on purpose, my life feels heavenly. And when I'm not, life can be utterly hellish. Do you want to be in heaven or hell? You have a choice.

The Realm of Angels and Other Light Beings

In addition to earthly assistance from family and friends, you have a vast array of heavenly guides that are available to team with you so you can maximize your ability to achieve your desired results. For many of us, it may be hard to ask for help. This is especially true if you see yourself as strong, self-sufficient, and successful in your own right. Societal norms suggest that needing assistance is a form of weakness. Yet the truth is that there is strength in numbers, in unity and in the power of team.

Who is included in this team of divine guides? I'm primarily talking about the hierarchy of angels, so let's start there. You may already know at least something about angels, even if you have not necessarily believed in them or sought their guidance. You don't have to subscribe to any religion to believe in the existence of angels and other light beings. The term "angel" is more of our earthly human word for these multi-dimensional beings of light that serve as protectors, guardians, divine messengers, and more. The study and understanding of the nature of these beings is deep and complex. For purposes of this book, I provide general information about particular angels that relate to each of the Seven Sacred Flames.

I have not only studied the angels for many years, but have deeply connected with them through prayer, meditation, and other intentional practices such as journaling and reading oracle cards. Oracle card decks, which differ from the more ancient and structured Tarot card decks, usually include images, words, or messages that vary in size and symbolic theme and are used as a focusing device for life situations at hand. Oracle angel cards are one of the easiest tools that I employed years ago to get to know the angels and seek Divine understanding. I particularly like the many decks created by Doreen Virtue, one of the most prolific and well-known experts on angels, with whom I have also studied. Once I became more familiar with the many angels, I began to include particular ones in my prayer petitions and journaling exercises. This has been a profound and increasing source of wisdom and power for me; the more I practice these ways, the clearer I become about the messages I receive, just as I am when I talk regularly to a particular person and know and recognize his or her voice.

I am a channel for Divine messages, particularly from the angels. I've known this for quite some time and have been intuiting messages from them and other beings in the heavenly realm. A few years ago, I met with my friend and colleague Sage Taylor Kingsley-Goddard, who is a channel for Archangel Michael and an Intuitive Abundance, Life Purpose & Business Acceleration Coach, for a series of spiritual mentoring sessions. In one session, Sage channeled a message for me directly from Archangel Gabriel, which she wrote out for me. I was not at all anticipating this, and when I read the message, I was in such awe that I cried.

Archangel Gabriel speaks:

"Dear One, I AM here. I AM all within you. I AM so much a part of you, at times you could not see or feel me. Can you see your own nose? You cannot see yourself unless you expand your vision. See yourself as others see you rightly. Then you will see your great gifts.

"I have an invitation for you. Actually, your language does not have a proper word for it. The word 'mission' comes close, as does 'sacred pact.' I would like for you to be one of my emissaries on earth. I open to you; you open to me. You know me quite well already. Feel the energy in these words. You have a choice. Part of you already said YES! I celebrate this!

"Part of you is wondering and worrying whether being my emissary will change you too much or make you strange, maybe even lose your will. Not to worry, dear child of God! Nothing could be further from the truth. I will, together with you, help you to be all of who you truly came here to be.

"You will feel different. More alive. More peaceful. More happy. More creative. More in the flow. More connected. More confident. So does this make you unusual among your fellow humans? Yes. Does it matter? Only if you allow it to.

"Would it be all right, all light to be a fearless, peerless leader even among Lightworkers? Would you like the RIGHT people to finally notice you and appreciate you? Would it be okay to fully claim your destiny? To touch thousands more people? To feel more joy in each moment? If you say YES to all of these, then you have your answers, as do I.

"Remember that one of my gifts to humanity and to you and through you is BALANCE. The black or white mentality, us versus them, and paradigm have never served you well. Multiplicities, integrations, expansion, diversity, collaboration, oneness AND independent source-fueled love power—now that is the new way to be! You and I together will model this.

"You are here to provide Archangel Activations, particularly of me (with me) and also Archangel Raphael. The work you/we came here to do focuses on CREATIVITY, Freedom, Expression, Joy, Balance, and Wholeness. There is a sense of EXPANSION and PEACE to all of this, your experiences with me, and what we call forth to bring to and through others. A sense of awakening wonder. I LOVE YOU so very much."[20]

This was yet another amazing validation of the mission I came here to serve. So, I did say yes, but I wasn't active about it for a while—and I admit I felt guilty that I was holding back. It did feel a bit too much. I could certainly handle the creative expression part—I'd already been doing that. But Archangel Activator? Really? According to the Bible and Catholic teaching, Archangel Gabriel is the angel that appeared to Mary to deliver the message of her Divine mission to birth Jesus, the Son of God, into the world. Now here this angel was, delivering a message for me. What if I wasn't able to deliver? Yet, I realized and acknowledged that if I am here to guide you in your full expression of self, then I can't hold back any longer in serving this aspect of my soul mission.

So I finally decided to come out of the angel closet and incorporate teachings from both Archangels Raphael and Gabriel into my writing, speaking, and coaching, as appropriate. And by revealing this message here, in this book, I'm really out of the closet now. This was certainly a huge aspect of my essence and gift that was suppressed when I worked in the corporate consulting world, as I'm sure you can imagine.

For purposes of The Destiny Designer™ methodology, here is a summary about the handful of specific angels that influence each of the Seven Sacred Flames, as I've gleaned from Virtue's decks and website and my own experience with these lightworkers, which does not preclude any other angel from influencing any aspect of your life at any time:[21]

∿ **Archangel Michael** – This powerful angel is a great warrior and protector–of your physical body, your spiritual destiny, and the expansion of your soul. He fights evil and champions you to transform any negative energy you feel or face into love.

∿ **Archangel Gabriel** – Known as the messenger of God, Gabriel lets you know what your Divine mission is and inspires your artistic communications. He is also powerful in resurrecting what appeared dead.

∿ **Archangel Raphael** – This Divine healer cascades powerful light and love medicine on everyone, as well as helps you manifest more love. Raphael also helps you to see your self and body as already whole and healthy, which magnifies the harmonizing effect of his intercession.

∿ **Archangel Jophiel** – This angel of illumination shines the light of beauty and creativity on all areas of your life, including your space and your inner and outer self.

∿ **Archangel Sandalphon** – This angel protects your earthly foundation and empowers you to face and conquer any fears you have for expressing your gifts, particularly when they involve music.

∿ **Archangel Metatron** – This angel is in charge of all metaphysical archives and is considered the secretary of God. He is a powerful agent to help you clear and purify your thoughts as well as understand enigmatic knowledge and concepts.

∿ **Archangel Zadkiel** – This archangel helps you focus your mind and heart on prayer invocations, especially when forgiveness is the focus, that keep you connected to the Divine as a natural practice.

∿ **Angel Hadraniel** – This heart angel of love helps awaken your memory of everlasting love, which is ultimately all that your soul needs to feel satisfied. He can help you nurture more love in your relationships.

∿ **Angel Ongkanon** – This angel can greatly assist you to enhance your communication with family members and other loved ones. He also provides deep understanding of strong feelings when they arise.

~ **Angel Paschar** – This angel helps you see beyond the material realm to inform your vision from the heavenly realm and your unconscious.

There are many other spiritual beings that you can call upon to be part of your spiritual power team such as Jesus Christ, the Holy Spirit, Mother Mary, Buddha, and others. Some refer to this group of light beings as Ascended Masters, or earthly humans who have achieved enlightenment. Others may consider any or all of them as part of their identification of God. What matters most is how you can tap the teaching or energy of any or all of them to awaken your own spirit and Life Plan. You can create affirmations or prayers to these angels and other light beings, and they can become part of your team just as you would incorporate teamwork in your business or family. You don't have to navigate your life journey alone. Finally, the spirits of your deceased love ones can be available to you for wisdom and guidance. Many people I know think about how a beloved one who has passed away may handle a situation when they are faced with it in order to help solve it or at least get through it with more ease.

The Realm of Natural Elements

The natural elements also play a significant role in generating and controlling the flow of energy and in activating each of the Seven Flames. Intentionally engaging with the elements maximizes your ability to design, manifest, and live your Divine Destiny. The elements of earth, water, fire, and air influence the first four chakras; the upper chakras are associated with the cosmic elements of ether, light, and spirit. The elements have their own properties and are also interconnected. In addition to finding ways to surround yourself with natural elements often, there are powerful ways you can incorporate them in transformational rituals, along with tools from the other realms. I give you some suggested practices in Chapter Six.

Earth

Earth, the foundation upon which you can manifest and build the life you desire, grounds you in the here and now. This element of purpose and presence–your foundation–represents the first chakra. Earth, which is solid, dense matter, matters to living your Divine Destiny.

How? When your body is grounded to the earth and your spirit resides in your body, you experience a fuller sense and feeling of "who I am," which enhances your ability to know what you're here to do and your power to carry it out. Your spirit can sometimes dwell near but outside of your body, especially if you have ever experienced physical trauma, or are someone who (like many of us) tends to reside in your mind and spirit more easily than in your body and on the ground. I have memories of my mother exclaiming to me, "Lauren, if your head was not attached to your body, it would just float away!" She didn't know that was my way of escaping our sometimes chaotic, though also loving, home environment. Fortunately, I learned the practice of how to intentionally connect with earth and nature, and to ground myself, which has been essential to solidifying my path to success.

Mother Earth is fertile and naturally abundant (without getting into current concerns about our human impact on this source). When I visualize just the crops alone that are needed to feed seven billion people on this planet, I am awestruck that the Earth can support this! The element of earth also relates to service, and Earth has been serving us for millions of years, and still is, so far.

Earth is a source of amazing beauty. I am grateful to have been able to explore so many natural wonders of majestic mountains, verdant valleys, meadows abundant with wildflowers, rich green forests, and more. I feel more alive thinking about being amid these earthly places. Sometimes, I need to remind myself that I can simply walk out my door, put my bare feet on the grass, and touch the trees right around me.

Earth is associated with the season of winter, the darkness of night, and the direction of North. Of course, Earth has a warming energy and gravitational power, which, thankfully, prevents any of us from floating off into the air and beyond, even when we are in hanging out in mind and spirit.

Water

Water, the element of creation and love, is associated with the second chakra. It represents your ability to be emotionally expressive in a balanced and effortless way, and to be playful. Water is connected with curiosity, and if you're willing to dive down a little below the surface to see what's there, you may be surprised at what you'll find.

Because water is fluid and formless, it facilitates and guides the natural flow and unfolding of your path. As Emerson suggested in his *Essays: First Series*, "Place yourself in the middle of the stream of power and wisdom which animates all whom it floats, and you are without effort impelled to truth, to right and a perfect contentment."[22] The ride can be amazing and exhilarating, or simply peaceful.

Water is awakening, cleansing, and refreshing. Don't you just love to stand in the shower and feel it wash over you, especially when you are particularly groggy upon getting out of bed? How about a dip in a lake or the ocean, on a hot, sunny day? And there's nothing like a cold glass of water to quench your thirst. Your own tears can water your soul. As American poet John Vance Cheney wrote in his 1892 poem *Tears*, "The soul would have no rainbow had the eyes no tears."

Water is also powerful. Running rivers and melting glaciers can carve canyons through mountains. Tsunamis and floods can create or destroy beaches and beyond. Ocean waves carry so much power that science is now capturing it to use as a newer alternative source of energy. Water is associated with the season of autumn, the time of dusk, and the direction of West.

Fire

Fire, the element of your personal power, spirit, and of the third chakra, is active; it moves and can spread quickly when unleashed. Fire is about connection—and its energy connects us. This blazing element is associated with the hot season of summer, the time of midday when the sun is brightest, and the direction of South. If you desire warmth, light, and a spirit of camaraderie, there's nothing cozier than sitting around a crackling campfire, or next to your stoked fireplace.

Fire burns away illusions, just as it burns away impurities. Gold is purified to its finest, most valuable state through an alchemizing process that uses fire. Sometimes, when you experience a trial in your life, it may feel like you are in a blazing inferno and that your feet are being put to the fire. Perhaps the trial is a refining process to help you burn away another illusion so you can become your brightest? Fire ignites and lights the way, and it can spark you to ignite your will and move your energy in the direction of your next steps for living your dream.

Air

Air is the element of the mind and the heart chakra, which also fuels the fire of passion. Air is expansive and light. The season of spring, the new dawn of sunrise, and the direction of East are each associated with this refreshing element. Like fire, air represents activity and movement. In addition to feeling refreshing, a nice breeze or wind can signify change and rebirth. Air is also associated with the intellect, so you can use your mind to intentionally set your direction and course and harness the energy of air's movement.

The Realm of Creativity and the Arts

How does your creative expression expand your ability to keep your inner fire burning and, beyond that, to live and play fully in your life? Many pioneers of expressive arts practices see imagination as the essence of the soul. Therefore, the intentional cultivation of the imagination is essential to bring about the soul's awakening and full expression. The active process of creativity is made even more transformational by allowing yourself to surrender to the unknown—the unconscious. It is when you learn to let go into the void of the unknown that new possibilities arise. You don't need to consider yourself "an artist" to be creative. We all have imagination—it is one of our six mental faculties.

In his book, *Minstrels of Soul*, expressive arts pioneer Paolo Knill characterizes the art disciplines as vehicles of and containers for the modalities of imagination—words, visual images, action, sound, rhythm, and movement. We communicate with these modalities all the time without the intention of "doing art" per se. Each art discipline also uses specific senses when we engage in it:

∾ Literature and poetry – auditory and visual

∾ Visual arts – visual

∾ Theater – auditory, sensorimotor, and visual

∾ Music – auditory

∾ Dance – sensorimotor

When you allow yourself to engage in different combinations of the visual arts, dance, music, writing, drama, and ritual art disciplines, you can uncover symbolic imagery that evokes new and changed perspectives about your own life conditions. What makes the creative process transformational versus art for art's sake is the intention to apply or carry the change or insight into the world and your life. Each of the Seven Sacred Flames offers a suggested creative practice for deepening and activating its essence.

Each art discipline can be powerful to help shift specific challenges. For example, if you feel stuck on an emotion or issue, a dance movement may help you move past it or discharge the energy around the pain. When you're feeling scattered or lost, a language arts process such as journaling may help you understand a narrative in your life and its patterns. If you are filled with emotions, chanting or drumming may help you express them in a primal, nonverbal way and get grounded. Painting or other visual arts help you create form around that which you're having difficulty making meaning. And dramatic role-play may help you see and release stuck patterns in any relationship.[23]

This could sound merely like great theory. Yet I stand on the experienced shoulders of all the pioneers of this field–

and Archangel Gabriel—who have awakened spirit through creativity. And I've experienced firsthand how the intentional practice of these disciplines work with clients in uniting a team around a common goal, getting a new insight, releasing a resentment, and more. As a therapist and a life coach, I've facilitated nearly one thousand hours of teambuilding and healing groups, as well as playshops in which I weaved together these art disciplines into exercises. I have a stream of memories and images of client transformations flowing through my mind like a movie as I write about this now.

Years ago, I created and facilitated expressive arts and drama therapy groups for recovering alcoholics in an inpatient treatment facility. The groups included a wide mix of people from many walks of life, some of who were initially skeptical about my creative processes. Soon enough, I was able to gain their trust by creating a safe environment for them to have fun and access buried feelings, thoughts, hopes, and dreams. It didn't take long for them to eagerly pick a colored scarf or a symbolic image card to represent how they were feeling. In one group session, we were all happily dancing to evocative music. Moments later, when a certain song came up next, one man literally broke into waves of tears as an old memory broke free. This gave him the opportunity to feel and express his repressed emotions, opening the way for healing. Play and creativity freed him in a way that simply talking about his life could not.

This wisdom is not new to current times. The practice of creative expression goes back a long way, nearly to the beginning of human life when primitive man etched images in his cave dwelling where he surely also danced and howled his story. Art is rooted in ritual activity, which is to celebrate the sacredness of life and human potential.

In ancient times, movement and dance rituals were used to express feelings and help discharge the stress of life. Dance and music were associated with divinity and healing. The Egyptians believed the goddess Isis sent music to humans to help them cleanse their souls. The Greeks worshipped Apollo as the god of music and medicine, and his son Asclepius ruled over the healing arts that they thought refreshed the soul. Pythagoras's teachings about universal harmony highlighted music as a means to align the body with the soul and the Divine. Plato and Aristotle both believed in music's power for influencing the entire human self.

Symbolic imagery is yet another dimension of the creative realm. Jung was the first psychologist of his time to understand the transforming power of images for the path to Self-actualization. Tarot or other oracle cards are powerful tools for working with symbolic imagery and archetypes. While there are some who use them as a fortune-telling device, I have found it to be more potent when used as a map to explore the current archetypal themes surrounding you and your life. There are many styles of Tarot and other oracle card decks, but most of them commonly depict an image on each that represents a specific concept.

ACTION: New Ways to Play

∿ **Play with Unconditional Love.** Identify a person in your life with whom you either have conflict or negative feelings. Let's say it is difficult for you to feel or act loving toward this person. Now, find one aspect of this person that you can appreciate. Consciously focus only on this trait whenever you think of or interact with this person.

∿ **Play with Nature.** Connect with at least one of the natural elements every day—inside or out and about. Feel your bare feet on the earth or sit against a tree. Take a walk near a beach, lake, or stream and observe or touch its flow. Feel the breeze as you walk along and notice your breath. Light a candle and gaze into its flame. How do you feel?

∿ **Play with Your Imagination.** Set aside time to engage in your imagination and the arts. Find a song that expresses a message that resonates for you—particularly one that may speak to an aspect of your truth that you have been holding in. Play the song and sing along with it. Create your favorite cuisine. Dance and move to your own groove. Paint a picture. Get an oracle deck and spontaneously pick a card every day.

CHAPTER 6

DELIGHT YOUR SEVEN SACRED FLAMES

Don't fear the light within.
May it ignite the Sacred Flame in your soul.
~ Paulo Coelho

We've been exploring a methodology for living, leading, and working with greater spirit, purpose, passion, and personal power so that your life and your success feels much more filled with and driven by your soul. As I have proposed, and so many other spiritual teachers agree, your soul contains a sacred flame, which is the light of your essence, or your unique spark of the Divine. In Part One of The Destiny Designer™ methodology, we explored how to spark your sacred flame by discovering the nature of your essence and your soul mission, by getting clear about your passions and by praising, and claiming your personal power. These are keys to activating your drive and desire.

In Part Two of The Destiny Designer™, we're now on the way to keep your flame burning. You've cleared that way by releasing physical stuff, people, resentments, and any other unfinished business that may have been dimming down your flame. Next, I'll guide you through Seven Sacred Flames that, when consistently fueled, will help you sustain YOUR soul's flame.

Activating your Seven Sacred Flames is an integral component of The Destiny Designer™ methodology, which, as I said earlier, combines wisdom and practices from chakra energy and light channels, nature's elements, angelic guidance, creative arts processes, and symbolic and archetypal imagery. Each of the Seven Sacred Flames carries a quality or principle that is essential to living your Divine Destiny, and each can be energized and sustained by aspects of the universal sources of energy and light discussed in Chapter Five.

Flame 1 Presence ~ Transform Fear and Be Here

Presence is your central foundation for grounding the visions and dreams you have for your life, which is essential for making them manifest. It is associated with the first, or root, chakra. The root chakra is the very foundation of your core survival (health and prosperity), family (tribe) association, and basic trust for existing. This is about feeling grounded in the here and now, about believing–and KNOWING–you have the right to be here, and about serving the particular purpose you were born to. When you live in the present, you can use all your senses, including your intuition, to notice signs from the Divine and to fill you with energy and spirit.

When you're not present, it is because you're likely living in your head, often either in the past or the future. It's fine to reminisce about past times in your life, as long as you're not stuck living there in any kind of regret over something you did or didn't do, or fantasy wish that things were still like those good ol' days. At the same time, it's also powerful to have the capacity to envision future possibilities, as long as you're not spending an inordinate amount of time worrying about things that *might* happen then. Living in a chronic state of fear can be detrimental to your health. Presence, mindfulness, and love can transform fear into positive fuel to activate and maximize your body's natural healing power. I love this ancient Sanskrit poem, attributed to Kalidasa, who was said to be one of the greatest of the Sanskrit dramatists. It speaks so eloquently to living in today:

"Look to this day:

For it is life, the very life of life.

In its brief course

Lie all the verities and realities of your existence.

The bliss of growth,

The glory of action,

The splendour of achievement

Are but experiences of time.

For yesterday is but a dream

And tomorrow is only a vision;

And today well-lived, makes

Yesterday a dream of happiness

And every tomorrow a vision of hope.

Look well therefore to this day;

Such is the salutation to the ever-new dawn!"[24]

Many philosophers over time have spoken of the power of presence, including Thich Nhat Hanh, the Dalai Lama, Ram Das, and even Jesus, who, according to the Bible in Matthew 10:7, said, "The kingdom of heaven is at hand." I believe what Jesus meant is that heaven is not some nirvana place in the sky, but a state of awareness of all that is good in the here and now. Today IS a gift. Give yourself the gift of practicing how to be present and in your body so you can create and experience your own heaven, right here and right now.

Signs of Flame 1 balance: Feeling stable, trusting, centered, and connected to yourself and others. Having abundant physical energy and the ability to actually sense it in your body.

Signs of Flame 1 blocks/imbalance: Feeling anxious, fearful, or off balance. Experiencing low back pain or other health problems. Having difficulty generating money for your basic needs.

New Ways to Fuel and Balance Flame 1

Access Angelic Wisdom. If you want some aid strengthening your foundation, call upon Archangel Sandalphon, who can also help you aim more of your power in Flame Three. You can craft a specific prayer request or even find an image of him to place near you.

Ground into the Earth Element. Practice meditation on a consistent basis. Here is one I learned from an intuitive consultant that I have found to be very powerful:

Place both feet firmly on the ground and your hands face up gently on your lap. Take three deep breaths, inhaling through your nose and exhaling through your mouth. Speak your name out loud three times. Intend for your feet to completely open up to Mother Earth and greet her. Invite earth's grounding energy to flow up through your feet into your body, slowly rising up your ankles, calves, and thighs and swirling around your first chakra root center. Now envision and intend for some of this energy to flow back down to the center of the earth, grounding you, as some of it continues to flow up through your naval, your solar plexus, your heart, your throat, your shoulders, and down your arms to your hands. Imagine the energy filling every cell in your body. Tune into your body and sense if you can feel this energy. If you don't, trust that after some practice with this, you will be able to physically feel this energy.

Activate an Archetype. The Tarot's Major Arcana archetypes that are particularly related to this flame include **The Empress** and **The Emperor.** The Empress is like Mother Earth, nurturing fertility and natural beauty. The Emperor is the solid and structured father figure. If you have a tarot deck, find these cards and focus on both the imagery on them and the message.

Play with the Arts. Do some drumming–it's a powerful and simple source of grounding and creating a steady beat for intention and purpose. Even if you do not have a drum, you can use any number of items in your midst, such as sticks, a pot, or the like. You can also identify and listen to music that exudes a powerful beat. One song I listen to for grounding and balancing Flame 1 is "Tribal" by Benise. Surround yourself with the red color of this chakra.

Flame 2: Play ~ Create and Re-create

Play, pleasure, creativity, and sexuality are all primary ways to pump your juiciness factor, your feelings, and sensations. They are associated with the second, or sacral, chakra, which is also about the balance of male and female aspects of self and your ability to be in communion with and honor another.

Water is the element of play and creation. It represents your ability to be emotionally expressive in a balanced way.

Remember that feeling of freedom and joy you felt when you were a kid from simply playing, whether on your own or with friends and family? I can still recall running around the neighborhood with my friends for hours, making up games, doing cartwheels, splashing in a sprinkler, climbing trees, building forts, playing softball, catching fireflies—whatever our imaginations conjured up. It was pure exhilaration! What if you could do so again with the joy and abandon you had as child? You are designed to have fun. Jesus said, "Truly I tell you, unless you change and become like little children, you will never enter the kingdom of heaven."

You don't need to lose your capacity for play as an adult!

At its underlying essence, play is really about having a sense of wonder and curiosity about the world around you. Play elicits excitement and exploration. It is about allowing yourself time to frolic or create, just for fun, without an end goal in mind. Too often, when you become an adult, you tend to lose your playful attitude toward life, which can add to any feeling of dispassion you might already have. You can bring a playful attitude to just about anything you do, even things that aren't "play" activities, to get your zest back.

If Flame 2 is out of balance, you can make an intention to engage in more play and recreational activities. I happen to love hiking in nature and walking on the beach or by the bay, just to name a couple of things. When my playtime is out of balance, I start to feel a little flat. That's when I know I need to get out and play. One afternoon last month, I went to the public golf course with my life partner in Tilden Regional Park, which is literally less than fifteen minutes from home. We had decided to go hit some balls at the driving range as neither of us had swung a club in many years. We both felt fabulous afterward, and wondered why we don't go up there more often to play some golf and explore all the other wonders in these beautiful nature grounds.

Play can also involve creative expression. Do you tend to judge your creative abilities? I can't tell you how many times I have heard an adult exclaim, "I don't have a creative bone in my body!" Creative expression is NOT about being "an artist," or making products that will sell in fine art stores—although if this is your desire, I urge you to consider this possibility.

The creative process itself mirrors the natural cycle of creation that generates all life forms. This void of the unknown is where the cycle of creativity begins and ends and begins again. Let me tie this back to the natural elements. Consider the element of water: in its formlessness lies all the possibilities for a new idea to emerge and rise into the mind's element of air where breaths of inspiration and desire shape it further. This idea needs to be grounded to the earth element so it can actually take physical form in the material world. Eventually, there is a letting go of it with the fire element where it can cycle back to the formless void all over again. Engaging in the arts is life giving.

Let's not forget about sexuality and its expression, which accesses this same juicy creative realm that generates aliveness. Sexual, spiritual, and creative energy come from the same source and help you connect to your life source.

Signs of Flame 2 balance: Feeling vibrant and joyful, having balanced moods, flowing easily with creativity.

Signs of Flame 2 blocks/imbalance: Feeling empty or flat, having mood swings, experiencing hip pain, blocked creative expression.

New Ways to Fuel and Balance Flame 2

Access Angelic Wisdom. If your creative expressions feel blocked, ask Archangel Jophiel to help you clarify the vision of what you desire or want to create.

Splash with the Water Element. Connect with water. Take a walk near a beach, lake, pond, or stream. Observe and even touch its flow. Luxuriate in a hot bath.

Activate an Archetype. *The Fool* possesses the impulse to embark into the unknown. This Major Arcana archetype represents innocence, frivolity, and creating something new.

Play with the Arts. Watercolor is a perfect art discipline and medium for you to sustain this flame. Try not to be concerned with the picture that shows up on your page–this is more about immersing in a very fluid form of colorful expression. Incorporate some orange hues into your piece, which is the color of this chakra, or simply light an orange candle while you paint. Listen to music that evokes a playful mood for you, or a song from your childhood. I recently listened to some songs from *Mary Poppins*, just for fun.

Flame 3: Power ~ Aim Your Inner Authority

People who can harness their inner authority are clear about their core values, which you rediscovered in Chapter Three, and they can align their choices and actions with those values. They are decisive and willing to be accountable for their actions rather than blame others for problems, and, because of this, they earn respect from their peers and those they lead. These masters of power are less interested in exerting control over others and more in influencing and empowering right actions toward desired results with others.

Your personal power is associated with the third chakra and the element of fire, which sparks you to ignite your will and move your energy. You already know now–if you didn't before–that you have immense power within. You've already begun to spark your power by naming and praising your essence. You've also begun to claim your right to access and use your inner authority. When you sustain this flame, you can aim your confidence in any direction you choose.

Your inner authority comes from multiple sources. First, as a spark of the Divine, it comes from your connection with that Divine source, the Universe, God, all that is–however you define it. Second, it comes from your own energy field and life force energy. The more you learn how to mobilize this source and connect it to and through all our chakras, the more powerful you will feel. Third, there is huge power in your emotions, which, of course, is *energy in motion*. Therefore, it is crucial to recognize and express your feelings as they arise. Finally, your inner power comes from knowing your purpose, along with your talents and gifts—and confidently owning them.

Signs of Flame 3 balance: Easily digesting all that you take in, having a solid sense of purpose, exercising your will, and being decisive and cheerful.

Signs of Flame 3 blocks/imbalance: Experiencing stomach or digestive issues, lacking confidence, being indecisive and frustrated.

New Ways to Fuel and Balance Flame 3

Access Angelic Wisdom. Sandalphon can help you strengthen your personal power and face and conquer any fears you have for bringing forth your gifts and talents.

Fuel with the Fire Element. Do a "Breath of Fire" exercise for a minute, which is powerful, rapid breathing from the solar plexus. Visualize a fiery ball of energy in your belly as you breath in and out through your nose only, with mouth closed, and see it expanding with each out breath. Many speakers and actors use this technique to pump up their power before they perform.

Activate an Archetype. There are two Major Arcana characters that carry the archetypal energy of this Flame. ***The***

Chariot symbolizes driving your will forth in victory, while *Strength* is about your ability to channel your courage to do so.

Play with the Arts. Do a dance or just move your body, either in the comfort of your private space, outdoors, or out at a club. Explore moving at different levels as a flame of fire does. Feel the burn in your body. If you aren't currently able to play with dance or movement, you can listen to or sing a song that expresses owning your power or feeling strong in who you are. Sometimes, I like to sing "I Am What I Am" (from La Cage aux Folles); even though it's about a gay character owning his essence, I relate to belting out those powerful lyrics. You can also draw or paint a self-portrait—whether literal or abstract—and color the various aspects of your image with hues that represent the different parts of you, including the yellow color of this chakra.

🕯 Flame 4: Passion ~ Open Your Heart

Let's get to the heart of the matter. Passion and love are the central powers for your body and spirit. You've already discovered that they are key pointers to and results of living your purpose. To take it further, these emotions are centered in your heart, so further opening your heart will sustain them. Passion is associated with the fourth chakra and the element of air. Air is expansive and light, as is love. Air can also fan the flame of a fire as well as your fourth flame.

That's why it is important to practice deep breathing as part of your daily practice. If you've experienced any trauma or wounding in your childhood or even later, you may have unconsciously learned to breathe in a shallow way. It's also easy to breathe this way if you feel fearful or you're still running the rat race. So let's take a pause right now and take three deep breaths. Doesn't it feel great?

Your heart is the meeting place or bridge where body and spirit are synthesized–both physically and metaphysically. In your physical life, when the heart is open, it literally pumps life-giving blood and oxygen throughout your body. If there is a blockage, you could have a heart attack, the heart could stop beating, and well–we all know what that means! From a metaphysical perspective, when your heart is open, you easily feel unity, compassion, and love.

Love is the opposite of fear. Fear, along with unforgivingness, will keep your heart closed. These states, caused by painful experiences, can form a cage of steel around your heart, dulling your light and constricting the flow that fires your passion. You already explored forgiveness as a necessary part of clearing your space. Now determine if there is still a cage around your heart and decide if you're ready to break it open.

There came a time in my life when I became acutely aware that my heart felt encaged. This was not obvious to outside observers–I was passionate, social, and outgoing. Yet, somehow, I knew that there was something almost physical around my heart that prevented me from fully feeling and being. Through all my personal development processes, I was pretty certain I knew why my very young child self had caged her heart—betrayals too difficult for a little heart to bear.

I had done a lot of healing work, including speaking my truth, yet the cage was still intact. It was time to deepen my forgiveness for those who I felt had betrayed me in some way. With the help and witnessing of supportive community, I created a self-revelatory theater ritual for unchaining my heart and marrying my spiritual self. It was powerful, and I felt more open and infused with love.

Still, years later, I discerned that my heart was not quite completely open. As with most awakening journeys, there are many layers to peel away until you really get to the heart of the matter. So I met again with Sage and my core heavenly team for what turned out to be a huge heart opening session, through further forgiveness of ancient happenings. During this session, I received a sacred invitation from the poet and philosopher Rumi, whom I love, as channeled by Sage.

"Find the pool of infinite wisdom within your own heart.
Drink deep of the nectar you find there.
Fill yourself with the Light that has no end."[25]

I share this with you so you can affirm this same wisdom for yourself. Your heart is filled with the Light that has no end. That is where your spark of the Divine resides.

Signs of Chakra 4 balance: Feeling empathic and connected to yourself and others, radiating love and light.

Signs of Chakra 4 blocks/imbalance: Experiencing heart or lung disease, inability to empathize, feelings of loneliness.

Access Angelic Wisdom. *Rafael* and *Hadraniel* are two loving and healing angels that can help you regenerate your heart so that it opens wider.

Activate an Archetype. The tarot archetype of *Temperance* activates the lesson of achieving a balanced heart. *The Hermit* can model how to spend time searching inward for realization. *The Lovers* archetype can help you explore love, devotion, and union.

Play with the Arts. Write a poem that expresses a heartfelt emotion. If the idea of writing a poem sounds challenging, you can start one by simply using a word or name, and then writing a phrase or sentence that begins with each letter in your chosen word. Since this flame carries the element of air, you can exercise your breathing by playing a musical wind instrument such as a recorder or flute, if you have one, or just by whistling. Surround yourself with the green color of this chakra.

⸙ Flame 5: Pledge ~ Speak Your Truth

Have you ever noticed that some people just seem to have the gift of gab? You may even be one of them! This ease of speech could depend on what you are speaking about. Perhaps it's easier to talk about topics that are not personal or that don't require you to take a stand and put a stake in the ground?

On the other hand, there are those times when you intend or want to say something, and the words just don't come out.

You might get choked up—the words get stuck in your throat. Or you may simply be at a loss for words and essential messages slip away. Your self-expression is related to your fifth, or throat, chakra, and the element of ether, which exists in the upper heavenly regions of the sky. The ether element provides the air space to allow your words to come out more freely and divinely.

When your fifth flame is in balance, your ability to speak your truth and manifest your goals and desires is accelerated. Purification is another aspect of this flame, because if you've cleared out the imbalance in the lower chakras and flames, you can infuse the expression of your highest truth with purpose, passion, and love.

Your throat is not just a center for communication, but also for *action*. In order for anything to happen, it must pass through the throat to become a reality. To activate and live your Divine Destiny, it is essential to make and keep pledges—to others and yourself. When you make a pledge, it is an oath, a promise to undertake something. You can start by making a pledge to know your truth and clearly speak it. And you can pledge to be discerning and selective about the pledges you make, which is enabled through purifying your space as you did in Chapter Four.

Signs of Chakra Five balance: Taking responsibility for what you say, speaking with confidence and self-expression, being musically inclined.

Signs of Chakra Five blocks/imbalance: Having sore throats, experiencing difficulty in expressing feelings, having the tendency to over or under commit, not keeping promises or commitments, self-censoring.

Access Angelic Wisdom. If you want to refine your communications, *Gabriel* and *Ongkanon* are the angels you can call upon from the realm of the lightworkers. Whether it has to do with your artistic expression or finding and speaking your truth to a friend or family member, you can call upon either or both of these powerful angels.

Activate an Archetype. *The Hierophant*, known as the wise teacher or priest, is the tarot archetype that can help you hone your spiritual philosophy and truth, and express it.

Play with the Arts. Sing a song that speaks to an aspect of your truth that you have been holding in. Play the song and sing along with it, or even just sing it a capella. Lately, I've been singing "Can't Keep it In" by Cat Stevens. Use a pen or, to be even bolder, a marker, that is blue, the color associated with this Flame, to write a letter in which you communicate something you want to say to somebody–even if you don't send it to that person.

⚫ Flame Six: Perception ~ Expand Your Field of Vision

Perception is yet another one of the six mental faculties that all human beings have, and if you use it wisely, can help build the life of your dreams. Perception is about awareness and focus. It entails using all the senses, including your sixth sense of *intuition*–which itself is another mental faculty.

Consciously, you can choose how you perceive something–both the good and the bad of it–since there is a duality in all things. Learning and practicing to *choose* how you want to perceive things and where you want to place your focus is essential in manifesting the goal, dream, or destined life you desire. Remember . . . where your mind goes, the energy flows. Thoughts are forms of energy, and they have a magnetic quality to them; the nature of your thoughts attracts things of like form. This is a key construct of the Law of Attraction. When I kept thinking repeatedly how I would die if I remained working at a job that I hated, I fed the thought its power and attracted a potentially fatal disease. Conversely, I've been thinking recently how deeply I desire to travel to Italy again because it's been so long since I had been there. So the other day, I followed an intuitive nudge to stop what I was doing and check flights. At that moment, a super low-fare flight came right into my lap. Thoughts and perceptions are powerful manifesting forces.

When you are able to strengthen the capacity of your "third eye," or sixth chakra, you're able to go beyond perception through the five senses of sight, smell, touch, taste, and hearing to "seeing" more possibilities and visions beyond the material realm. We naturally knew how to engage this mental faculty when we were kids, and it may take practice or training to remember how to do so as adults. But it is possible and powerful. Light is the element of perception and the sixth chakra. I know some people who are considered clairvoyant, which means that their third eye is totally open, and they have vision beyond our three-dimensional material world. They can literally see spirits, angels, and more, sometimes even if they don't want to. Yet, you don't have to have clairvoyance to be able to activate your perceptive abilities so that you can intuit and envision more possibilities for you life.

Signs of Flame Six balance: Living an inspired life, accessing and applying inner and divine wisdom, feeling hopeful, trusting your intuition, believing in possibilities.

Signs of Flame Six blocks/imbalance: Experiencing headaches, not trusting yourself or other wisdom, feeling hopeless, or losing hope.

Brighten Up with the Light Element: Visualize an indigo ball of light in the center of your forehead while meditating.

Access Angelic Wisdom. If you want a new perspective on an aspect of your life, ask *Archangel Paschar* to help you see beyond what seems obvious about it to your naked eyes. He can also help you see your dream vision more clearly, as well as see the perfection in what you already have in your life. If you want some extra powerful clarity about how your soul mission really looks, call upon *Archangel Michael.* He will also be a warrior protector over the evolution of your destiny.

Activate an Archetype. *The High Priestess*, sometimes known as the Queen of the Underworld, can help you tune into your intuition and inner depth. You can also infuse the intuitive and magical energy of *The Moon* to expand your field of vision.

Play with the Arts. Shoot some nighttime photos with any camera you have, including your smart phone. It could feel particularly magical to use the moonlight as your lighting. Notice how your perspective may change in this light.

🕯 Flame Seven: Prayer ~ Align with the Divine

Prayer is the utmost way for you to stay connected with your purpose, vision and truth. Prayer is about establishing a communication–both calling out for and receiving information and guidance–from your own inner wisdom and with some power greater than yourself. The power greater than yourself can be associated with a particular deity or religion, but, again, it does not have to be. As Gandhi said, "There is no god higher than truth."

A prayer comes from a deep call from your heart, along with a focus from your mind. The more it is connected with desire, the more intense and powerful the prayer will be. Your personal form of prayer needs to feel authentic to your style of connecting and to elicit peace and joy–essential states for being aligned with the Divine. Spirit is the element of the crown chakra and of prayer.

Prayer doesn't have to occur in church, at your beside, or only in times of trouble. Prayer is also about cultivating a consciousness or awareness of the divine throughout your daily activities. The more you acknowledge this presence everywhere and anywhere, the more divine and illuminated the world will seem and be.

Signs of Chakra Seven balance: Feeling connected with spirit, sleeping through the night, asking for guidance and for your desires, being fair-minded, reverent, and peaceful.

Signs of Chakra Seven blocks/imbalance: Interruption of sleep/wake cycle, having nightmarish dreams, feeling disconnected from your body and/or Source, being intolerant.

Access Angelic Wisdom. Befriend *Archangel Zadkiel* to further cultivate your reverence for life, and enhance your ability to both speak and hear your prayer conversations.

Explore a Tarot Archetype. *The Star* and *The World* archetypes can expand your faith and hope in the face of anything, reminding you that a new cycle of potential, development, and achievement will always come around again.

Play with the Arts. Create an altar in an area of your home where you feel comfortable dedicating to your connection with spirit. Place a white or violet candle on it, along with other items that you associate with the Divine or spiritual world. These can include stones or crystals like amethyst or clear quartz, angel image cards or statues, tarot cards, crystals, anything that feels right to you. Spend time at your altar as you are guided. The good energy will build at the altar and within you.

How Fiercely Bright Are Your Flames Now?

Now that you've learned more about the Seven Sacred Flames, you can assess your current state of brightness in each of your own. Based on the signs for identifying your state of balance and imbalance discussed above for each Flame, use the image on the following page to color in the current brilliance of each of your Flames. It might help to actually take a copy of the image if you don't want to mark up your book. You can also download this image from my website at www.LaurenPerotti.com. Be as creative with this as you want by using a variety of colors and shapes.

Once you have a vision of your radiance, note what specific practices you can incorporate from the above section to further ignite or balance those Flames that need some support. In Part Three of The Destiny Designer™, you will discover how you can then playfully and prosperously shine your light out in the world.

Your 7 Sacred Flames Assessment Tool

PART THREE

Shine Your Light

Do not feel lonely, the entire universe
is inside you. Stop acting so small.
You are the universe in ecstatic motion.

~ Rumi

CHAPTER 7

March Confidently in the Direction of Your Dreams

Wherefore seeing we also are compassed about with
so great a cloud of witnesses,
let us lay aside every weight, and the sin which
doth so easily beset us,
and let us run with patience the race that
is set before us.
~ Hebrews 12:1

I trust you see your mission and your dream with so much more clarity than when you began this process. It's now time for you to shine your brilliant, unique, genius light out in the world, on your path. This next phase requires commitment, confidence, courage, and, most importantly, action steps. It's time for you to be in ecstatic motion. When you have witnesses that are cheering you on to move forward, it becomes even more inspiring and easier to take those actions that will manifest what you've been visioning and building toward in the process.

Your witnesses are your cheerleaders. They include those who have already bridged the gap from their pleasure-less plateau to the pleasure island they saw on the other side of what seemed like an abyss. They are your own core heavenly team in another dimension from this earthly world. They are family and friends who understand and see your vision and want to see you start living it. They could be fellow members of a mastermind group. Your biggest cheerleader can be a mentor or life coach who guides you to keep believing and marching forward when it seems as if nothing is happening.

All it takes is a step in the direction of what you've discovered that you desire more of in your life. You're blazing a new path. Sometimes, you may walk or stroll along the way, while other times you really want to skip or run. On this path, you get to choose your pace: to pause for play, for refueling, and to enjoy the landscape all around you. This is not about getting *to* a destination at which time you'll then be happy. It's about setting out on your path, with renewed energy and empowerment, with your clear vision and noticing what you begin to attract to you.

Regardless of what literal ways you actually take your steps, inwardly you are marching. When you march, you hold another attitude and energy altogether. It can be that of celebration, excitement, honor, and even triumph. This is why towns and cities all over the world hold marching parades past cheering witnesses to memorialize an occasion. This is why soldiers march in lock step to remain focused on their mission or, afterward, to return home in victory. Remember when I shared how inspired I felt by the Triumphal March scene in the opera Aida that I first saw in Italy? Marching exudes confidence and courage. First, you need to make a commitment to what you want.

Commitment

Commitment is an act of entrustment to give entirely to a specific person, activity, or cause. When you commit to your dreams through actions, you communicate to yourself, the universe, and others that you intend to realize them. You create the energy vibration and forward movement necessary for dreams to manifest. Engaging this mental activity can propel you down your success path.

The mental ability to make wise, sound decisions is one of the most fundamental skills any person can develop in order to maximize personal or business success. Bob Proctor, considered by many to be a master teacher of the Law of Attraction, has said that the powerful mental faculty of deciding, when engaged, can help nearly eliminate conflict and confusion and maximize success and income. All you need to do is look at your results to get a gauge on your decision-making strength.

When you decide, you bring order and integration to your mind, both of which are energies that create. When you vacillate in indecision, doubt, or ambivalence, you literally facilitate disintegration.

You may tend to commit to too many things. It's easy to say yes and sometimes hard to say no, maybe even to yourself. This often generates a lot of busyness, and can give the appearance that you are accomplishing things, which may truly be the case—sometimes. But too often, you may commit to situations, projects, or events that are not really connected to your goals, dreams, or highest good. On the other hand, there are those times when you DON'T commit to something you may be the most passionate about becoming or being involved in.

Your decision-making ability can become thwarted by any number of factors. Fear—of the unknown, of making the wrong decision, or of losing the choices you pass up once a decision is made—may be top on the list. Another factor may be information overload when faced with too many choices. Fear and overwhelm are frequently related to escape and avoidance, which can paralyze any progress or goal achievement in your business and life.

Courage and Confidence

Courage is often associated with bravery, boldness, fortitude, and even fight. A common societal association for courage is of war soldiers on the battlefield—risking their lives for the cause of protection and freedom. A universal symbol of courage is the lion, king of the forest. The lion in the *Wizard of Oz* believed he didn't possess courage and wanted the wizard to grant it to him. Yet, this cowardly lion boldly confronted the fear involved with facing the wicked witch to try to capture her broom, as the wizard commanded was necessary before he'd consider granting this request.

Courage is not the absence of fear, but the quality of spirit that confronts fear, pain, danger, uncertainty, or intimidation while continuing along your path. Regardless of facing or having faced opposition or perhaps failure, you keep marching. Courage is both a virtue and an act that is impelled by the desire to obtain or accomplish more. The practice of making courageous acts encourages growth and blossoming.

The core of the word itself comes from the Latin word for heart. In days gone by, that was also a common association for courage. If some desire, cause, or purpose burns in your heart, it can fuel your aspiration to go forward no matter what obstacles you may encounter. And if you don't move the obstacle, it may just remain there and cause you heartburn! The more confident you are in yourself, your purpose, and vision, the more courage you will have to face whatever it takes to live the life you are imagining.

Connection

As John Donne said, "No man is an island, entire of itself; every man is a piece of the continent, a part of the main." We can't do it alone—we need community! Think of community as your dream team of sorts that mutually supports one another and keeps each moving forward. I have spoken with so many people who expressed how difficult it was to reach out and ask for help, or talk to others about what they were going through during challenging times. Yet when these people did connect to a community or even a single other person, they described feeling validated, supported, and enlivened. It is often in the collaboration of a group mind–the mastermind–that new dreams emerge.

Live the Life You Imagine

Let me take you back to a time when certain people learned ways of thinking to get beyond conditions to materialize dreams and goals. As I learned from Mary Morrissey, a group of writers and thinkers like Emerson, Alcott, Hawthorne, and Thoreau came together in the mid 1800s at Emerson's home in Concord to mastermind their dreams. Emerson had read in the Bible that Jesus told his followers they could do the same and even greater things as he was doing in his ministry, which included manifesting miracles. He wondered if Jesus really meant that, and, if so, how could anyone do so?[26] Emerson wanted to gather with others whom were just as curious to explore possibilities for realizing big ideas. Concord was the place where the American Revolution started, so it already carried a spirit of forging new dreams.

These gatherings became known as the Concord Conversations, which stimulated new thinking and access to deeper self. Some people consider this early mastermind group as the gateway to modern psychology and the human potential movement.

Thoreau eventually decided he didn't just want to talk about these great questions they were exploring, but to test them. He embarked on an experiment to live in a small shack he built on Walden Pond for exactly two years, two months, and two days so he could discover what it felt like to live deliberately and with intense presence in the here and now in his surroundings. Just like I felt in the crucible of my crisis of meaning, when it came time for Thoreau to die, he didn't want to discover that he had not been living.

Four days into his experiment, Thoreau soon realized that he had created a grooved path to the lake because he walked that same way every day. He wondered how often he did this same thing in his life. At the beginning of this book, you already explored how easy it is to live on autopilot, to keep on doing the same things, the same way, every day. I find it amazing that Thoreau chose to conduct his experiments for that specific period of time. Thoreau was obviously deep and intuitive, and I don't believe this was accidental. As you already know, there are many ways I work with numbers, so when I learned about this years ago, I pondered about what the meaning that the number two, and the triple of the number two, might have been for Thoreau.

In numerology, this number carries the energy of peace and is associated with pursuing life purpose and soul mission.

Also, the master number 22 is one of the most powerful as it is supports building dreams into reality. Through a spiritual communication lens, the angels often use numbers to get our attention and communicate to us from the heavenly realm. According to Angel Therapist Doreen Virtue, the number 222 is a message of encouragement to keep nurturing your idea or dream as it is growing into reality. Perhaps Thoreau was aware enough about the interpretations that he consciously used these numbers to determine how long he'd try this?

Thoreau wrote his book *Walden; or Life in the Woods,* which I've already mentioned earlier, at the end of his experiment. He shares one of his most potent findings in the book's conclusion, which includes a frequently excerpted inspirational quote about advancing in the direction of your dream. The full clause says this:

"I learned this, at least, by my experiment: that if one advances confidently in the direction of his dreams, and endeavors to live the life which he has imagined, he will meet with a success unexpected in common hours. He will put some things behind, will pass an invisible boundary; new, universal, and more liberal laws will begin to establish themselves around and within him; or the old laws be expanded, and interpreted in his favor in a more liberal sense, and he will live with the license of a higher order of beings. In proportion as he simplifies his life, the laws of the universe will appear less complex, and solitude will not be solitude, nor poverty poverty, nor weakness weakness. If you have built castles in the air, your work need not be lost; that is where they should be. Now put the foundations under them."[27]

It sounds lofty and inspiring, doesn't it? You've probably encountered at least some part of this quote before. However, what you may not know is that if you are able to drill down to what Thoreau is actually saying, you will find a code for creating and living a life you love. I learned the key to unlock this code from Mary Morrissey's *DreamBuilder Program*, and I want to show you how it can work for you. I'll start at the beginning.

Just like Thoreau, you want to enter into an experiment with what's possible for your life when you live with more purpose and passion, maybe even more simply. To say that "**If**" you do so implies that you have a choice. You don't **have** to endeavor to do anything differently. If you have a choice, then you have both freedom and responsibility. The experience of your life is up to you and not anyone or anything outside of you. You are not a victim but an activator of your life. If you find yourself using the phrase "I have to . . ." about anything, try to catch yourself and reframe your language to that of personal choice.[28]

Your advance is fueled by confidence, which I just talked about above. It obviously doesn't mean you won't feel fear once you step forward in a new direction, but because you have faith, you do it anyway. This advance can begin with something as simple as buying and reading this book, and then engaging in the suggested actions at the end of every chapter.

All you need to do is to endeavor, which simply means try it out. You do need a direction, though, unless you want to sail around in circles or end up wherever the wind takes you. This can be fun for a while, but not forever if you have goals.

Set your direction fresh each day with your vision-driven thinking. Thoughts create reality. Everything that exists in the material realm began first as a thought. That's why they are so powerful, even though they are invisible. When you shift your ways of thinking from condition-based limits to a focus on possibilities–and take action–you pass an invisible boundary. That's when the magic starts to happen. The universe responds by turning the wheels to bring people, situations, and opportunities to you that match your thoughts and vibration. Theses things would not have occurred had you not advanced in that direction.

As Thoreau discovered, vision-driven thinking helps you to manifest your dreams. Once you begin to practice this new way of living, you will become more aware of how simple it is to tap into universal wisdom to now accomplish many new successes. It might feel different at first, but you will enjoy the freedom to set your intention and follow the direction of your choice. You have all the elements available to ground your dreams on this earth.

ACTION: New Ways to Play

~ **Make a Decision.** Make a list of all your major commitments, past and present, and rate them on a scale of both how much of your energy they consume and how relevant they are to your burgeoning vision and dreams. Determine if there are any of which you can let go. Most importantly, add to the list those that are relevant but missing. Make a decision to commit to them.

~ **Mastermind with Like-Minded Others.** Form or join a group of like-minded others to connect with, even if it's over something as simple as a meal. If you are already part of a group or community, consider making it into a masterminding resource for all of you.

~ **March One Step Forward.** Reflect on a time when you took an action on something even when you felt fearful or unsure about doing so or about the outcome. It could be as simple as sharing in a large group. How did you feel afterward? Identify one act that you may be procrastinating and imagine you actually doing it. Use feelings from your past experience to fuel your confidence and courage. Then do it!

CHAPTER 8

MAKE A LIFEPLAY PLAN

Before I can tell my life what I want to do with it,
I must listen to my life telling me who I am.

~ *Parker J. Palmer*

At this point, you shouldn't be surprised that a chapter talking about making a plan is toward the end of this book, and even **after** you've already begun to march confidently in the direction of your dream. Most traditional programs would have you make a plan first. Your LifePlay Plan will be that much more infused with your spirit, because by now, you've discovered who you are, clarified your impassioned dream vision, and activated it by taking action steps into the unknown. As I just talked about in Chapter Seven, this is where the universe and the Divine co-create miracles and magic with you.

That's not to say that The Destiny Designer™ methodology is linear, or that you have to do it in the order presented. The cycle of creativity is circular, and the universe is spiral and expanding, so this process can work in that way too. It is something you can come back to over and over again.

Now, you can make a LifePlay Plan by putting together the ingredients you've discovered that will make your life a masterpiece. It's always powerful to put ideas and designs in writing, therefore I suggest you do so with your plan. You can craft it in any format you want, but here is a simple way to lay it out.

Your Name

My Essence

My Soul Mission

My Passion and Dreams

My Top Core Values

Talents that MUST be Expressed

My Core Team

Spiritual beings

Earthly beings

My Best Practices for:

Being present

Playing

Aiming my Power

Opening my Heart

Speaking my Truth

Perceiving Higher Wisdom

Aligning with the Divine

My Commitments

My Mastermind Group

This LifePlay Plan can be a living, evolving blueprint, as you will continue to change, along with the people and the world around you. One of the most important things to remember is that you don't stop dreaming, and that WE won't stop dreaming.

CHAPTER 9

MAGNETIZE YOUR PLAYFUL PROSPERITY

Doing what you love is the cornerstone
of having abundance in your life.

~ Wayne Dyer

There is a magical synergy that occurs when you begin to activate the Seven Sacred Flames with all the universal realms on a consistent basis. Together, there is a mindset, which is an elemental, energetic, creative shift–sometimes subtle, sometimes sudden–that opens a conduit to rain down abundance on your path and on you!

This abundance is not solely about financial wealth and money, though it can be. Money is just another form of energy that you can attract through your spirit-centered, joyful pursuits. Prosperity is a state of being rather than a state of having. This state of being is most possible when all of your aspects of self and soul are activated, open, flowing, and expressed—and vibrating at a high level. The more you keep that flow moving and circulating by giving and sharing, the more there is for you to receive, and then give again. This is one of the laws of the Universe.

The law of giving and receiving is about the harmonious exchange of all the elements of the universe with one another and with you. That means that in order for all this energy to keep flowing, there needs to be a balance in both giving and receiving. You may feel more comfortable giving than receiving, or vice versa. The ability to strike a healthy balance between giving and receiving with others and with your resources is a hallmark of spirit-centered living and leading, which magnetizes prosperity.

When you are living your LifePlay Plan, you will experience so much more laughter, joy, and lightness of being than you ever have before, or at least more than you have in a while. When you add gratitude to that mix of ingredients, your feeling of abundance can be overflowing. These are all treasures that can light your path to the success you desire. While you play along your yellow brick road on the way to Oz, may you discover even more treasures, along with the wisdom, to recognize that what you are seeking has been within you all along—growing and glowing the more you share it and let it shine. Therein lies your true gold.

CLOSING AND CONTINUING

Congratulations for taking the journey all the way to the end of this book! It has been an honor and a joy for me to present this wisdom to you, and my hope is that you've already had at least one revelation just by reading it. No matter how deep you dove into this material in your reading, the beauty of The Destiny Designer™ methodology–and the Seven Sacred Flames in particular–is that you can return to it and use these tools throughout your life as your journey continues. I want your playful path to continue as well.

That's why I also created a three-part virtual PlayShop from the wisdom presented in this book. Of course, the deeper you immerse in The Destiny Designer™ process as a way of being and living, the more your life vision will unfold for you to live in amazing and fun ways. I've found that in order to really effect change that makes a lasting difference, it is most helpful to have a structured program to follow over a period of time so that you create a new habit. As I discussed in Chapter Seven, when you also have a community of like-minded people with whom you can check in and share your experiences, your transformation will be even more empowered.

To discover more about this, visit www.LaurenPerotti. com.

ACKNOWLEDGEMENTS

I want to express my heartfelt gratitude and thanks to many people who contributed to the creation of this book. Special thanks goes to Richard Unger and the International Institute of Hand Analysis for permission to incorporate his vast wisdom about Hand Analysis here.

Special thanks also goes to Mary Morrissey and the Life Mastery Institute for permission to incorporate wisdom from the *DreamBuilder Program* and *The Vision Workshop: Living Your Life Full Spectrum* in this book.

My acknowledgment and thanks goes to Thomas R. Allen for permission to use his original fractal artwork titled *Follow the Yellow Brick Road* as the cover design for this book.

My deep appreciation and accolades goes to Daren Heldstab Photography (www.darenheldstab.com) for providing his fabulous photographs of me for use here.

Finally, to my family and friends who encouraged me and gave me helpful feedback along the way.

Thank you!

Lauren

ENDNOTES

Quotes and certain other wisdom from the following wonderful books and resources have also been included in this book:

Chapter 1

1. The Myers & Briggs Foundation. (2014). MBTI® Basics. Retrieved March, 2016, from http://www.myersbriggs. org/my-mbti-personality-type/mbti-basics/.
2. The Myers & Briggs Foundation. (2014). The 16 MBTI® Types. Retrieved March, 2016, from http:// www.myersbriggs.org/my-mbti-personality-type/mbti-basics/the-16-mbti-types.htm.
3. The Bible, Revelations 21: 10 – 23 (NIV).
4. "Learning About Numerology," accessed October 2016, http://www.numerology.com/numerology-news/learning-about-numerology.
5. The Enneagram Institute, last modified August 26, 2016, accessed October 2016, https://www.enneagraminstitute.com.

6. "Signs of the Zodiac," last modified 2016, accessed October 2016, https://cafeastrology.com/articles/signsofthezodiac.html.

7. International Institute of Hand Analysis, last modified 2014, accessed October 2016, http://www.handanalysis.net/index.html.

8. American Academy of Hand Analysis, 2015, accessed October 2016, http://academyofhandanalysis.org.

9. Richard Unger, *LIFEPRINTS: Deciphering Your Life Purpose from Your Fingerprints.* (Berkeley: Crossing Press, 2007), 28-32.

10. Richard Unger, *LIFEPRINTS: Deciphering Your Life Purpose from Your Fingerprints.* (Berkeley: Crossing Press, 2007), 33-36.

11. Richard Unger, *LIFEPRINTS: Deciphering Your Life Purpose from Your Fingerprints.* (Berkeley: Crossing Press, 2007), 37-41.

12. Richard Unger, *LIFEPRINTS: Deciphering Your Life Purpose from Your Fingerprints.* (Berkeley: Crossing Press, 2007), 42-46.

13. Richard Unger, *LIFEPRINTS: Deciphering Your Life Purpose from Your Fingerprints.* (Berkeley: Crossing Press, 2007), 1-6.

14. Richard Unger, *LIFEPRINTS: Deciphering Your Life Purpose from Your Fingerprints.* (Berkeley: Crossing Press, 2007), 7-8.

15. Richard Unger, *LIFEPRINTS: Deciphering Your Life Purpose from Your Fingerprints.* (Berkeley: Crossing Press, 2007), 7-8.

Chapter 2

16. Mary Morrissey, *The Vision Workshop: Living Your Life Full Spectrum.* (Los Angeles: Life Mastery Institute, 2012), 9-13.

Chapter 4

17. Author Unknown, "Reason, Season, or Lifetime," last modified March 1, 2009, accessed October 2016, https://lifelessons4u.wordpress.com/2009/03/01/are-you-a-reason-a-season-or-a-lifetime/.
18. Gay Hendricks, *The Big Leap: Conquer Your Hidden Fear and Take Life to the Next Level.* (New York, NY: HarperCollins, 2009).

Chapter 5

19. Bible, 1 Corinthians 13: 8-13 (NIV).
20. Sage Taylor Kingsley-Goddard, Channeling of Archangel Gabriel for author.
21. Doreen Virtue, AngelTherapy, 2016, last accessed October 2016, www.angeltherapy.com.
22. Ralph Waldo Emerson, *Essays, First Series,* Project Gutenberg Etext, December 2001, last accessed

October 2016, www.scribd.com/document/253319733/
Ralph-Waldo-Emerson-Essays-Firsr-Series-1894.

23. Paolo J. Knill, Helen Neinhaus Barba, and Margo N. Fuchs, *Minstrels of Soul: Intermodel Expressive Therapy* (Toronto, Ontario: Palmerston Press, 1995), 32-34.

Chapter 6

24. Kalidasa, "Look To This Day," accessed October 2016, https://allpoetry.com/Kalidasa.

25. Sage Taylor Kingsley-Goddard, Channeling of Rumi for author.

Chapter 7

26. Mary Morrissey, *The Vision Workshop: Living Your Life Full Spectrum.* (Los Angeles: Life Mastery Institute, 2012), 3-5.

27. Henry David Thoreau, *Walden or, Life in the Woods* (Walden Pond: Internet Book Mobile, 2004), last accessed October 2016, http://www.eldritchpress.org/walden5.pdf.

28. Mary Morrissey, *The Vision Workshop: Living Your Life Full Spectrum.* (Los Angeles: Life Mastery Institute, 2012), 5-7.

ABOUT THE AUTHOR

*The more she tells her story, the more she
can let go of it. As she keeps changing the
story, the story keeps changing her.*
~ Paolo Knill

Lauren Perotti is an international bestselling author, transformational speaker, and *Dream*Builder Coach. Lauren blends over thirty-two years of expertise in business, psychology, and the arts together with her passion and her creative approaches to guide professionals to align their lives and livelihoods with their highest vision and life purpose. Lauren knows firsthand that when you ignite the fire of your purpose, passion, and power, you can truly make your life a masterpiece in ALL realms—without sacrificing your soul! By teaching her clients how to tap into universal sources of energy, imagination, and

Light, they are able to free their creative spirit and experience playful prosperity and discover how to be vital forces in a new era of leadership that allows spirit, imagination, and creativity to inform strategies, decision, and actions.

Lauren holds a Master's Degree in Counseling Psychology and Expressive Arts Therapy and a Bachelor's Degree in Accountancy. She is a Life Mastery Institute Certified *Dream*Builder Coach as well as a Doreen Virtue Certified Angel Card Reader. She's worked with people and businesses from a wide variety of spectrums through individual and group coaching as well as live workshop and playshop forums. She also happily uses her business acumen serving as the Chief Financial and Strategy Officer for a prominent family-owned Napa Valley vineyard and real estate group of companies.

Lauren is an advocate for living your passion. From her home in the San Francisco Bay Area, she lives her own passion by traveling with her sweetheart, writing, speaking, and singing. While skipping along her Yellow Brick Road, Lauren meets and leads others to discover that, on their way to Oz, what they seek is already within them.

For more information on Lauren, please visit LaurenPerotti.com.

YOUR NOTES

YOUR NOTES

. . . .

89568285R00109

Made in the USA
San Bernardino, CA
27 September 2018